KU-497-822

# CONTENTS

# Useful information for readers

Dear Reader,

### *Issues: Drugs in the UK*

Although the use of most illegal drugs has fallen since 1998, figures remain worryingly high, particularly among young people. In addition, the easy availability of a wide range of substances means that dangerous drugs such as ketamine and crystal meth are becoming increasingly popular. This book looks at trends in drug use, the effects of different drugs and the law surrounding drug use.

### The purpose of *Issues*

**Drugs in the UK** is the one hundred and sixty-third volume in the **Issues** series. The aim of this series is to offer up-to-date information about important issues in our world. Whether you are a regular reader or new to the series, we do hope you find this book a useful overview of the many and complex issues involved in the topic. This title replaces an older volume in the **Issues** series, Volume 114: **Drug Abuse,** which is now out of print.

Titles in the **Issues** series are resource books designed to be of especial use to those undertaking project work or requiring an overview of facts, opinions and information on a particular subject, particularly as a prelude to undertaking their own research.

The information in this book is not from a single author, publication or organisation; the value of this unique series lies in the fact that it presents information from a wide variety of sources, including:
⇨ Government reports and statistics
⇨ Newspaper articles and features
⇨ Information from think-tanks and policy institutes
⇨ Magazine features and surveys
⇨ Website material
⇨ Literature from lobby groups and charitable organisations. *

### Critical evaluation

Because the information reprinted here is from a number of different sources, readers should bear in mind the origin of the text and whether the source is likely to have a particular bias or agenda when presenting information (just as they would if undertaking their own research). It is hoped that, as you read about the many aspects of the issues explored in this book, you will critically evaluate the information presented. It is important that you decide whether you are being presented with facts or opinions. Does the writer give a biased or an unbiased report? If an opinion is being expressed, do you agree with the writer?

**Drugs in the UK** offers a useful starting point for those who need convenient access to information about the many issues involved. However, it is only a starting point. Following each article is a URL to the relevant organisation's website, which you may wish to visit for further information.

Kind regards,

Lisa Firth
Editor, **Issues** series

*Please note that Independence Publishers has no political affiliations or opinions on the topics covered in the **Issues** series, and any views quoted in this book are not necessarily those of the publisher or its staff.*

---

## ISSUES TODAY
### A RESOURCE FOR KEY STAGE 3

Younger readers can also now benefit from the thorough editorial process which characterises the **Issues** series with the launch of a new range of titles for 11- to 14-year-old students, **Issues Today**. In addition to containing information from a wide range of sources, rewritten with this age group in mind, **Issues Today** titles also feature comprehensive glossaries, an accessible and attractive layout and handy tasks and assignments which can be used in class, for homework or as a revision aid. In addition, these titles are fully photocopiable. For more information, please visit the **Issues Today** section of our website (www.independence. co.uk).

# Drugs in the UK

## ISSUES

## Volume 163

**Series Editor**

**Lisa Firth**

**Independence**

Educational Publishers
Cambridge

First published by Independence
The Studio, High Green
Great Shelford
Cambridge CB22 5EG
England

© Independence 2008

**British Library Cataloguing in Publication Data**
Drugs in the UK – (Issues Series)
I. Firth, Lisa II. Series
362.2'9

ISBN 978 1 86168 456 1

**Printed in Great Britain**
MWL Print Group Ltd

**Cover**
The illustration on the front cover is by
Angelo Madrid.

# Drugs in the UK

## Information from the Economic and Social Research Council

A drug is a chemical compound that can alter the way the mind and body work. Drugs can be natural or synthetic (man-made) and can be used for a variety of reasons including medical or recreational. Although foods and drinks have an effect on the mind and body they are generally not considered drugs as they are ingested for nutritional and sustenance purposes.

Alcohol, or drinks containing ethanol have been consumed since pre-historic times and plants containing drugs have been chewed and smoked for thousands of years.

### Medicinal drug use

Drugs are used widely for their curative, preventative or therapeutic properties. In the past, the benefits, or perceived benefits of natural botanical drugs were passed down through generations and cultures and natural medicinal drugs are still widely used in many societies.

Today the field of pharmacy is the application of chemical sciences for the use of medication. Pharmaceutical companies research, develop, market and distribute healthcare drugs. The industry is subject to many laws regarding the patenting, testing and marketing of drugs. In the UK, pharmaceutical companies are regulated by the Medicines and Healthcare Products Regulatory Agency (MHRA) and by the Medicines Act 1968.

The pharmaceutical industry is one of Britain's leading manufacturing sectors bringing in a trade surplus of £3.4 billion in 2004 with over £12.2 billion in exports as shown in Table 1. Two of the leading 10 pharmaceutical companies in the world are UK companies and own a market share of over 10 per cent.

### Recreational drug use

When a person's reason for using a drug is to obtain effects other than medical or therapeutic reasons it is known as recreational drug use. When an individual takes a drug occasionally rather than regularly, this is called casual use. The term implies that the user is not dependent or addicted, but it does not indicate the motive for use or the amount used on any occasion.

### Utilitarian drug use

Utilitarian drug use is when a person uses a drug for a specific benefit other than for medical reasons or personal pleasure. This might include the relief of fatigue or insomnia or the control of appetite. The lines between utilitarian use, abuse and misuse are hard to define and usually are dependent on the circumstance. Performance-enhancing drugs taken by athletes would be considered drug abuse whereas amphetamines used to increase a soldier's endurance generally aren't thought of as drug abuse.

### Drug abuse and misuse

The term drug abuse is difficult to define and carries different meanings in different situations. Some drugs, such as morphine, have medical purposes. If they are used for other reasons, or in unnecessarily large quantities, then the term 'drug abuse' is applied. Other substances, such as alcohol, are legal but do not serve a therapeutic purpose. Using alcohol to a degree that is hazardous or damaging, either to the user or to others, is also understood as abuse. Any use of illegal substances that have no recognised medical purpose is generally regarded as abuse. Thus the best general definition of drug abuse is the use of any drug in a way that does not follow medical advice or that does not conform to a particular culture's accepted usage. The term 'misuse' refers specifically to the use of a therapeutic drug in any way other than what is seen as good medical practice.

### The regulation and prohibition of drugs

Reasons for drug regulations are varied. In the UK in 1858, the Poisons Act was passed to control substances falling into the hands of criminals. In 1916 the passage of the Defence of the Realm Act (DORA) was a piece of emergency wartime legislation controlling cocaine and opium possession, distribution and sales with an emphasis on ensuring the availability of medicinal drugs when needed. In 1969 LSD was prohibited,

fuelled in part by hysterical media coverage over the growing counter-culture of the psychedelic music scene.

The history of drug legislation in the UK and abroad is not one of simple health protection. Indeed the UK Home Office states 'The distinction between legal and illegal substances is not unequivocally based on pharmacology, economic or risk benefit analysis. It is also based in large part on historical and cultural precedents.' This accounts for the wide sale and consumption of drugs such as alcohol and tobacco which also have related health risks but are viewed as socially or culturally more acceptable than many other drugs.

In the UK, the main piece of legislation covering drugs is the Misuse of Drugs Act first introduced in 1971. Offences under the act include:
⇨ Possession of a controlled substance unlawfully.
⇨ Possession of a controlled substance with intent to supply it.
⇨ Supplying or offering to supply a controlled drug (even where no charge is made for the drug).
⇨ Allowing premises you occupy or manage to be used for the purpose of drug taking.

To enforce this law the police have special powers to stop, detain and search people on 'reasonable suspicion' that they are in possession of a controlled drug.

## Drug classifications

The Misuse of Drugs Act groups drugs into various classifications termed as controlled substances. The classification uses an A, B and C grouping where class A is considered the most harmful, and therefore incurs the highest penalty.

Table 2 shows the penalties for possessing and supplying drugs in each of the different classes.

Table 1 gives only a selection of controlled substances. A full list of drugs currently controlled under the Misuse of Drugs Act is available.

## Types of drugs

The effects of drugs vary greatly and can alter the way a person thinks, acts or feels along with many changes in a person's perception of the world around them. Drugs are usually placed into three broad categories based upon their attributed effects:

*Stimulants (Uppers)*
⇨ Definition – Drugs that speed up or excite the central nervous system, and make you feel more alert and energetic, cause you to stay awake for long periods of time, decrease your appetite and make you feel good (e.g. relaxed, euphoric).
⇨ Examples – Cocaine/crack, amphetamines (speed), tobacco (nicotine), caffeine.

*Depressants (Downers)*
⇨ Definition – Drugs that slow down the functions of the central nervous system and make you less aware of the events around you.
⇨ Examples – Alcohol: beer, wine, distilled spirits. Opiates (painkillers): opium, morphine, heroin, codeine, methadone, Demerol, Percodan. Sedatives/hypnotic: barbiturates (Seconal), sleeping medications, Rohypnol (date rape drug). Tranquillisers: Valium, Librium, diazepam (anti-anxiety medications). Inhalants: paint thinners, shoe polish, glue.

*Hallucinogens (Psychedelics)*
⇨ Definition – Drugs that distort the senses and one's awareness or perception of events. One might hallucinate – seeing or hearing things that don't actually exist.
⇨ Examples – LSD (acid), PCP (angel dust, crystal, peace pill), mescaline (buttons), ketamine, magic mushrooms.

The categories above are broad and due to variations in the source of drugs, production methods, purity and individual differences in drug users, the effects of many drugs may not fall into any one category. Ecstasy for example is associated with being both a stimulant and a hallucinogen whilst cannabis can fall into all three categories. A psychoactive drug chart in the form of a Venn diagram is a useful way to understand the overlapping effects of many drugs.

## Taking drugs and drug addiction

Drugs can be administered in various methods – including orally, by inhaling or by injection – and each is an important factor in the reaction to the drug.

As well as the route of administration, many factors can affect drug reactions, such as dosage, setting and a person's tolerance to a drug or the placebo effect. The placebo effect is a psychosomatic effect where a user expects a certain effect from a certain drug and then experiences the desired results, even if the active ingredients to produce the results are not present in the substance. Cross-cultural research has also has shown that drugs can produce different effects depending on cultural variables.

Tolerance to a drug develops when the response to the same dose of a drug decreases with repeated use. Tolerance usually occurs with depressants, such as alcohol and opiates, but tolerance to amphetamines has also been found.

Addiction is defined by the World Health Organisation as the 'Repeated use of a psychoactive substance or substances, to the extent that the user (referred to as an addict) is periodically or chronically intoxicated, shows a compulsion to take the preferred substance (or substances), has great difficulty in voluntarily ceasing or modifying substance use, and exhibits determination to obtain psychoactive substances by almost any means'. The dependency on a drug can be either physical or psychological. Typically tolerance is prominent and a withdrawal syndrome frequently occurs when substance use is interrupted.

Withdrawal symptoms are users' reactions when they abstain from a drug they have become physically dependent on. Psychological and/or physiological reactions are usually the opposite effect of the drug and withdrawal from depressants can lead to restlessness, irritability, nausea and tremors.

## Drugs and crime

Between 2004/05 and 2005/06, all recorded drug-related offences increased by 23 per cent from 145,546 up to 178,502. Offences of cannabis possession rose from 88,056 to 119,922; an increase of 36 per cent. This increase in cannabis offences coincided with the downgrading of cannabis in January 2004 from a class B to a class C drug. In the light of new research, which linked the drug more closely to mental illness, the Home Secretary considered regrading it back to a class B drug, but decided against this in January 2006.

Drug-related offences accounted for 3 per cent of all recorded crime in England and Wales in 2005/06. However, drug use can be associated with other forms of criminal activity. For example, an addict may resort to theft if they are unable to pay for drugs. Although it is difficult to measure the links between drug use and offending, a Home Office project found that within a sample, around 65 per cent of those arrested tested positive for at least one drug and 27 per cent for two or more.

Although findings tend to suggest that drug use is associated with higher levels of prevalence (the proportion of the population) and incidence (the rate of offending of those involved) of offending, direct links between criminality and drugs are unclear. A wider association has been made, usually that drug taking leads to crime. This is often socially generated and fuelled in part by the media or anti-drug groups. In recent research by Glasgow Caledonian University a study of 126 users of heroin showed that it is possible to take heroin in a controlled way, with limited or no negative impacts on the user or society.

### Illicit drug use

It is estimated that 34.9 per cent (over 11 million) of all people aged 16 to 59 have used one or more illicit drugs in their lifetime. 13.9 per cent have used a class A drug and cannabis is the most likely drug to be used with 8.7 per cent, or roughly one in 12 people, having used it in the last year. Figure 1 below shows the prevalence of drugs use in 2005/06.

### Drugs and young people

The 2005/06 British Crime Survey estimates that 45.1 per cent of 16- to 24-year-olds have used one or more illicit drugs in their lifetime, 25.2 per cent (over 1 and a half million) have used one or more illicit drugs in the last year and 15.1 per cent in the last month, as shown in Figure 2 below.

The most widely used illicit drug for 16- to 24-year-olds is cannabis. British Crime Survey figures from 2005/06 show that 21.4 per cent had used the drug in the previous year, while 5.9 per cent had used cocaine, and 4.3 per cent had used ecstasy.

### Frequency of drug use

In 2005/06, 41.2 per cent of cannabis users regularly used the drug more than once a month compared with 22.3 per cent of cocaine users and 16.1 per cent of ecstasy users. Overall 19.9 per cent of class A users take class A drugs more than once a month. However, the overall figures for frequent drug use have fallen from 12.4 per cent in 2003/04 to 9.5 per cent in 2005/06.
*27 July 2007*

⇨ The above information is reprinted with kind permission from the Economic and Social Research Council. Visit www.esrcsocietytoday. ac.uk for more information.

© ESRC

## Drugs in the UK – statistics

Table 1: World trade in pharmaceuticals, 2004 (£billions)

| Country | Exports | Imports | Balance |
|---|---|---|---|
| Switzerland | 12,052 | 6,491 | 5,561 |
| France | 12,302 | 8,012 | 4,290 |
| Germany | 19,616 | 15,349 | 4,267 |
| UK | 12,354 | 8,642 | 3,712 |
| Sweden | 4,082 | 1,503 | 2,579 |
| Netherlands | 6,533 | 9,094 | 439 |
| Italy | 6,074 | 6,690 | 616 |
| Australia | 1,141 | 2,717 | -1,576 |
| Spain | 2,716 | 4,831 | -2,115 |
| Japan | 1,677 | 3,829 | -2,152 |
| Canada | 1,815 | 4,034 | -2,219 |
| USA | 11,989 | 19,099 | -7,109 |

*Source: 'Facts and statistics from the pharmaceutical industry (2006)'. The Medicines and Healthcare Products Regulatory Agency (MHRA).*

Table 2: Penalties for possessing and supplying drugs

| Class | Examples | Possession | Supply |
|---|---|---|---|
| Class A | Heroin, cocaine, LSD, ecstasy, methadone, magic mushrooms (if prepared for use), amphetamines (if prepared for injection) | Up to 7 years and/or an unlimited fine | Up to life in prison and/or an unlimited fine |
| Class B | Amphetamines, Methylphenidate (Ritalin), Pholcodine, Cannabis (from January 2009) | Up to 5 years in prison and/or an unlimited fine | Up to 14 years in prison and/or an unlimited fine |
| Class C | Cannabis (until January 2009), tranquilisers, some painkillers, GHB (Gamma hydroxybutyrate) | Up to 2 years in prison and/or an unlimited fine | Up to 14 years in prison and/or an unlimited fine |

*Source: 'Misuse of Drugs Act (2006)'. Home Office. Crown copyright.*

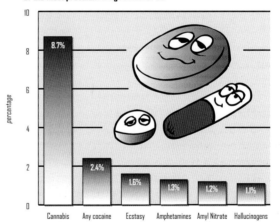

Figure 1: Percentage of 16-59 year olds reporting use of the most prevalent drugs in 2005/06

- Cannabis: 8.7%
- Any cocaine: 2.4%
- Ecstasy: 1.6%
- Amphetamines: 1.3%
- Amyl Nitrate: 1.2%
- Hallucinogens: 1.1%

*Source: Drug Misuse Declared (2006) The Home Office p10. Crown copyright.*

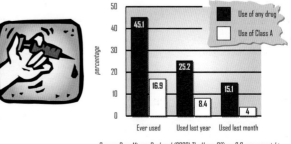

Figure 2: Percentage of 16-24 year olds reporting having used any drug or Class A drugs ever, in the last year and last month, 2005/06.

- Use of any drug
- Use of Class A

| | Ever used | Used last year | Used last month |
|---|---|---|---|
| Use of any drug | 45.1 | 25.2 | 15.1 |
| Use of Class A | 16.9 | 8.4 | 4 |

*Source: Drug Misuse Declared (2006) The Home Office p2 Crown copyright.*

# Information about common street drugs

## Information from Parents Against Drug Abuse

### The stimulant drugs

*Cocaine and crack cocaine*

**Source:** Derived from the coca plant, a bush native to countries in South America such as Bolivia, Chile and Peru. Cultivated in South America, South East Asia, Africa and Australia for the narcotic alkaloids of its leaves.

**Route of administration:** Usually by snorting whereby the drug is sniffed up a nostril through a tube. Can also be injected either by itself or mixed with another drug such as heroin (speedball). Cocaine can also be smoked using a process known as freebasing. Crack is a type of cocaine which is smoked in pipes having been prepared into a rock-like substance. Because crack has a far more transient effect than ordinary cocaine and consequently a higher 'buzz' users are more likely to escalate their usage to achieve the desired effect.

**What does it look like?** Cocaine is a white powder. Crack cocaine is found in the form of small, rock-like crystals.

**Effects:** It has a stimulant effect on the central nervous system: a pleasurable state of well-being, relief from fatigue, increased mental alertness, increased physical strength, reduction of hunger and indifference to pain. When snorted, effects peak after 15-30 minutes then diminish. Crack cocaine effects are immediate but shorter-lived (approx. 5 minutes).

**Problems:** Large doses can lead to agitation, anxiety, paranoia and hallucination, particularly hallucinations such as feeling things crawling over the skin. A state similar to paranoid schizophrenia may be precipitated by long-term use. Repeated snorting can damage the lining of the nose and the nasal septum. Injecting can lead to all the usual complications associated with injecting such as ulcers, abscesses, inflammation of the veins, endocartisis, tetanus, hepatitis and HIV infection. Causes increased heart rate, blood pressure and temperature. Overdose can cause death. Smoking crack can damage the lungs.

Neither tolerance nor withdrawal symptoms occur with repeated cocaine use, however psychological dependence can develop. This is more rapid in onset with freebased cocaine. Babies born to 'crack mothers' may be smaller, irritable, suffer tremblings and feed poorly, however the symptoms will disappear in a few days.

**Detectability:** Cocaine metabolites are detectable in urine for up to three days.

**Legal status:** Cocaine and crack are classified Class A drugs. Possession carries a sentence of up to 7 years' imprisonment and an unlimited fine. Supplying is punishable by up to life imprisonment and an unlimited fine.

**Some street names:** Base, Big C, Charlie, Coke, Dust, Koka, Snow and Stardust.

*Amphetamines*

**Source:** These are synthetic drugs having no natural base. They can be home produced.

**Route of administration:** Can be taken orally, by inhalation or by injection.

**What does it look like?** A powder which can be either white, yellow or pink in colour. It has an acrid taste and a slight odour.

**Effects:** Sought-after effects are wakefulness, mental alertness, increased initiative, elevation of mood, enhanced confidence, euphoria or elation, lessened sense of fatigue, talkativeness and increased ability to concentrate. Breathing and pulse rates are increased, pupils are dilated and appetite suppressed. Blood sugar levels are raised. Other characteristic symptoms are tremor, restlessness, agitation, sleeplessness, and reduced hunger. When swallowed effects may not be apparent for 30-60 minutes (this is decreased when the drug is inhaled or injected). Effects last for three to four hours. Tolerance can develop rapidly.

**Problems:** This drug can cause chest pains, palpitations, blurred vision and confusion. Users with pre-existing heart problems should avoid any stimulant drugs as results can be fatal. As effects wear off the user becomes restless, nervous and agitated. Depression may follow as may irritability, fear and aggression. Once sleep is achieved it is usually heavy but disturbed. Overdose or prolonged use of moderate doses can precipitate a form of psychosis which is characterised by delirium, paranoia, aggression and hallucinations as well as unpleasant side effects such as sweating, tremor, headache and insomnia.

## Drug groups

| Stimulants | Depressants | Hallucinogens | Others |
|---|---|---|---|
| ▸ Caffeine | ▸ Alcohol | ▸ LSD | ▸ Poppers |
| ▸ Nicotine | ▸ Barbiturates | ▸ Magic mushrooms | ▸ Steroids |
| ▸ Amphetamine | ▸ Benzodiazepines | ▸ Mescaline | |
| ▸ Cocaine | ▸ Opiates | ▸ Bufotenine | |
| ▸ Crack | ▸ Opioids | ▸ Harmine | |
| ▸ Ecstasy | ▸ Cannabis | ▸ Ketamine | |
| | ▸ Solvents | ▸ Phencyclidine | |

*Source: Parents Against Drug Abuse*

Overdose could be fatal.

Injecting amphetamines leads to the complications associated with that activity as described previously.

**Detectability:** Amphetamine metabolites are detectable in urine for between 2 and 4 days.

**Legal status:** All true amphetamines are considered Class B drugs. Possession is punishable by up to five years' imprisonment and an unlimited fine. Supplying is punishable by up to 14 years' imprisonment and an unlimited fine. If, however, amphetamine is prepared for injection, the increased penalties for a Class A drug apply.

**Some street names:** Amphet, Billy, Whizz, Speed, Poor Man's Cocaine, Uppers.

### Ecstasy

**Source:** True ecstasy is an amphetamine-type drug which should, more correctly, be called MDMA. This is a chemical similar to amphetamine. However, a high percentage of so-called ecstasy on sale today does not contain this substance, but rather a combination of other drugs such as amphetamine and LSD. Some tablets have been found to contain heroin. Most ecstasy in this country is imported from Holland although recently it is believed that it may be being manufactured in the UK.

**Route of administration:** Usually by mouth, although there are some variants.

**What does it look like?** Available in tablet or capsule form. It ranges from brown to white with pink, blue, red, black, white, yellow and clear options available.

**Effects:** There are a mixture of physical and psychological effects experienced by the user within 30 minutes to one hour of ingestion. Effects can last up to a maximum of 24 hours. Emotional changes include serenity, calmness, enhanced communication, benevolence, heightened sense of touch, empathy and understanding. There may be increased sensitivity to light, blurring of vision, difficulty in focussing, dilated pupils and involuntary movement of the eyes. Visual hallucinations are known but rare.

**Problems:** Negative effects include jaw-clenching, dry mouth, excessive sweating, blurred vision, inco-ordination of movement, nausea, anxiety, panic attacks, insomnia, depression and fatigue. There have been some deaths. Other side effects include acute liver failure or acute respiratory failure. There is growing evidence that long-term use can lead to liver damage.

---

## The opiates are the oldest group of drugs known to man

---

**Detectability:** Metabolites of ecstasy are detectable in urine for up to 4 days.

**Legal status:** Ecstasy is a Class A drug. Possession can lead to imprisonment of up to 7 years and an unlimited fine. Dealing can lead to life imprisonment and an unlimited fine.

**Street names:** E's, Disco Biscuits, Doves, Love drug, MDMA, Playboys, Tabs.

### The depressants

**Opiates/opioids**

**Source:** The opiates are the oldest group of drugs known to man. They are derived from the opium poppy which is grown in such places as Turkey, Iran, Afghanistan, Pakistan, India, Thailand, Burma, Laos and China. Opioids are synthetic drugs which resemble opiates in their effect. Opioids are available on prescription from doctors.

**Route of administration:** They can be smoked or injected and in some cases, snorted. Smoking heroin is known as 'chasing the dragon'. Many opioids are produced in tablet form.

**What does it look like?** Unadulterated heroin comes as a white pill which can be crushed to a fluffy, white powder. The majority of street heroin found in this country is a light brown powder, this is because of the adulterants used to make up the bulk. Methadone is an opioid which is used widely in the treatment of heroin addiction. It is marketed under the name Physeptone.

**Effects:** These drugs act on the frontal lobes of the brain. They are known to depress pain responses. Following administration results will appear in about 15 to 20 minutes with peak effect in 45-90 minutes. The effects are general central nervous system depression, reduction in pain perception, a reduction of fear and apprehension, warm feeling in the stomach, lessening of inhibitions, an expansion of ego and an elevation of mood.

**Problems:** The most dangerous problem is toxic reaction due to overdose. This is usually an acute, life-threatening event. Other complications are decreased respiration, cyanosis, nose running, constipation, pulmonary oedema and/or cerebral oedema. All opiates are capable of producing unpleasant withdrawal symptoms. Within 12 hours of the last dose there is usually the beginnings of physical discomfort characterised by watery eyes, runny nose, sweating and yawning. Within 12 to 24 hours the user will move into a restless sleep. Other symptoms including dilated pupils, loss of appetite, goosebumps, back pain and tremor will begin to appear. This in turn gives way to insomnia, incessant yawning, weakness, stomach upset, chills and flushing. There may also be muscle spasms, and abdominal pain. The acute phase of withdrawal will decrease in intensity and is usually greatly reduced by the fifth day, disappearing in one week to ten days. Tolerance to most opiates develops quite quickly and physical dependence can develop with relatively short-term usage. The degree of dependence varies according to the potency of the opiate/opioid used, the amounts taken and the length of exposure to the particular drug.

**Detectability:** Heroin and similar opiate metabolites may be detectable in urine for up to five days.

**Legal status:** Heroin and methadone are Class A drugs.

**Some street names:** H, Brown, Crap, Mexican Brown, Scag, Shit, Smack.

### Solvents

Any volatile substance which gives off fumes of an intoxicating nature may be the source of this habit.

**Route of administration:** Inhalation

is the most prevalent route of administration for solvents.

**Effects:** The effects of solvent misuse come fairly quickly, within seconds or minutes. They lead to lowered oxygen levels in the brain and disinhibition. The effects can be likened to alcohol intoxication but only last a very short time.

**Problems:** Feeling of dizziness, unreality, slurred speech, staggering and double vision. Some users may hallucinate. Continued inhalation can cause disorientation, drowsiness and sometimes unconsciousness, Some volatile substances are cardiac stimulants and the risk of cardiac arrest is high in someone who may have a predisposing heart condition. Prolonged bursts from aerosols can lead to 'freezing' of the breathing mechanism. There are increased risks of brain, nervous system, kidney, muscle, stomach and liver damage due to the toxicity of some chemicals used. Estimates put deaths from solvent abuse at 2-3 per week in Britain. Some evidence suggests that physical dependence can occur with solvent abuse.

**Detectability:** There are no specific tests available.

**Legal status:** Solvents are not illegal. The only legislation applies to the selling of solvents to anyone under the age of 18. Maximum penalties for this are a six-month prison sentence and/or a fine up to £2000.

### Cannabis

**Source:** Cannabis is derived from a bushy plant, originally from Central Asia. Most of the cannabis in this country is imported from North Africa, the Middle East and Asia.

**Route of administration:** Most common route is by smoking hand-rolled cannabis and tobacco (joints or spliffs). Other methods include smoking with a pipe known as a bong, eating in food or brewed as tea.

**What does it look like?** There are 3 types of cannabis – the dried, chopped plant itself known as 'grass' or 'bush'. This looks like dried grass/herbs. Cannabis resin is compressed into blocks which are dark brown in colour. This is known as hash and is generally stronger than 'grass'. Cannabis oil is made by percolating a solvent through blocks of resin. This is the most potent form of cannabis.

**Effects:** When smoked, the effects of cannabis are noticeable within a very short time. When eaten the effect takes longer. Intoxication lasts for between two and eight hours depending on the potency and the amount consumed. The user will normally experience relaxation, talkativeness, euphoria, bouts of hilarity and greater sensory stimuli such as tastes, colours, sounds etc. There may be an increased sense of hunger.

---

## LSD produces changes in perception ranging from illusions to full-scale hallucinations

---

**Problems:** Very rarely there may be nausea. Overdose is unknown, tolerance is insignificant and it is not addictive. However, some individuals may become psychologically dependent. There is no evidence to suggest that cannabis leads to the use of stronger, more harmful drugs. Cannabis can be dangerous to someone with pre-existing heart problems.

### The hallucinogens

**LSD**

**Source:** Derived from a fungus that affects grasses and cereal grain. It is manufactured illegally, and fairly easily, with the bulk being imported from Holland.

**Route of administration:** Usual method is by swallowing.

**Effects:** LSD produces changes in perception ranging from illusions to full-scale hallucinations. This response will depend on the user's personality, education, expectation and environment as well as the dose involved. The effect is said to be a psychedelic (mind-expanding) experience. Typical effects include an increased awareness of sensory input including colours, shapes and sounds; a subjective feeling of increased mental activity; altered body image; changes in sense of time and place and a difficulty in differentiating between one's self and one's surroundings. LSD takes effect within 30 minutes to one hour and lasts for up to 12 hours.

**Problems:** Panic reactions and paranoia are common problems. There may be loss of contact with reality, palpitations, severe perspiration and blurred vision. Psychotic reactions may occur, but these usually clear within a matter of weeks. Where there is a pre-existing disposition to psychiatric illness, the psychosis can develop into mania, depression or schizophrenia. 'Flashbacks' are a fairly common complication. This is when the user experiences the effects of LSD without actually taking it. No long-term dangers are known. Although they are not addictive, some users may become psychologically dependent. No significant withdrawal signs have been described and overdose is unknown.

**Detectability:** LSD metabolites may be detected in urine for up to three days.

**Legal status:** LSD is a Class A drug.

**Some street names:** Acid, Batman, Strawbs, Lucy, Trips.

### Magic mushrooms

**Source:** Derived from two types of mushroom which grow wild in Britain.

**Route of administration:** Ingested orally. May be smoked, cooked or brewed in tea.

**Effects:** Changes in perception ranging from illusions to full-blown hallucinations depending on the amount ingested. The user's personality, education, expectations and environment will also influence the effects. Gives feelings of increased mental activity. Effects very similar to those experienced with LSD.

**Problems:** Loss of contact with reality, palpitations, blurred vision and paranoia. As with LSD, flashbacks can occur.

**Detectability:** No specific tests available for magic mushrooms.

⇨ The above information is reprinted with kind permission from Parents Against Drug Abuse. Visit www.pada.org.uk for more information.

*© Parents Against Drug Abuse*

# Use of illicit drugs

## General population: extent of drug use and trends since 1998. From the British Crime Survey 2006/07

⇨ The 2006/07 BCS estimates that 35.5% of 16- to 59-year-olds have used one or more illicit drugs in their lifetime, 10.0% used one or more illicit drugs in the last year and 5.9% in the last month.

⇨ The survey also estimates that 13.8% of those aged 16 to 59 have used a Class A drug at least once in their lifetime, 3.4% used at least one Class A drug in the last year and 1.7% last month.

⇨ Cannabis is the drug most likely to be used. The 2006/07 BCS indicates that 8.2% of 16- to 59-year-olds reported using cannabis in the last year. Cocaine is the next most commonly used drug with 2.6% reporting use of any form of it (either cocaine powder or crack cocaine) in the last year.

⇨ Use of ecstasy in the last year is estimated at 1.8%, amyl nitrite at 1.4% and amphetamine use at 1.3%. The use of hallucinogens (LSD and magic mushrooms) in the last year was reported by 0.7% of 16- to 59-year-olds.

---

**It is estimated that just over 11 and a quarter million people aged 16 to 59 in England and Wales have used illicit drugs in their lifetime**

---

⇨ This is the first year that questions on ketamine have been asked in the BCS. Use of ketamine in the past year was reported by 0.3% of 16- to 59-year-olds.

⇨ It is estimated that just over 11 and a quarter million people aged 16 to 59 in England and Wales have used illicit drugs in their lifetime, while just under three and a quarter million are estimated to have used illicit drugs in the last year and almost two million in the last month.

⇨ It is also estimated that just under four and a half million people aged 16 to 59 have used Class A drugs in their lifetime with just over one million having used them in the past year and just over 500 thousand in the last month.

---

**35.5% of 16- to 59-year-olds have used one or more illicit drugs in their lifetime, 10.0% used one or more illicit drugs in the last year and 5.9% in the last month**

---

⇨ When looking at specific types of drugs, it is estimated that just over 800,000 people used cocaine powder and just over 550,000 people used ecstasy in the last year.

⇨ The proportion of 16- to 59-year-olds who used any illicit drug in the last year was lower in 2006/07 than in 1998, mainly due to successive declines in cannabis use since 2003/04.

⇨ There was no statistically significant difference between 2005/06 and 2006/07 in the overall level of any illicit drug use in the last year.

⇨ Class A drug use in the past year among 16- to 59-year-olds was higher in 2006/07 than in 1998. This is mainly due to a comparatively large increase in cocaine powder use between 1998 and 2000. However, between 2000 and 2006/07 the use of Class A drugs overall remained stable. The use of hallucinogens decreased overall between 1998 and 2006/07.

⇨ The figures for 2006/07, compared to 2005/06, show a stable pattern for all Class A drugs, with the exception of magic mushrooms which show a decrease in the past year.

*October 2007*

⇨ The above information is reprinted with kind permission from the Home Office and is an extract from the document *Drug Misuse Declared: Findings from the 2006/07 British Crime Survey England and Wales* by Rachel Murphy and Stephen Roe. Visit www.homeoffice.gov.uk for more information.

© *Crown copyright*

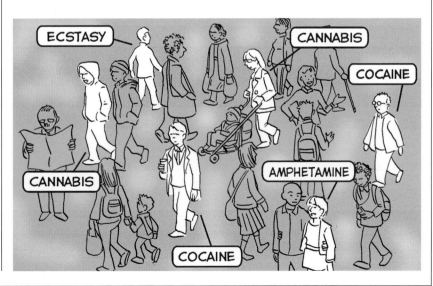

# Drugs: key facts

| | Class | More details | Estimated no. users | Users, % population | Average price | Deaths, 2006** |
|---|---|---|---|---|---|---|
| **Cocaine** | A | Slang: coke, Charlie, C, white, Percy, snow, toot<br>Appearance: white powder, often wrapped in small packets of paper or clingfilm<br>Taken: snorted up the nose or injected | 828,000 | 2.6 | £30-55 per gram | 190 |
| **Crack** | A | Slang: rocks, wash, stones, pebbles, base, freebase<br>Appearance: small lumps or rocks about the size of raisins<br>Taken: usually smoked in a pipe, glass tube, plastic bottle or in foil, or injected | 58,000* | 0.2 | £10-25 per rock | See note below** |
| **Ecstasy** | A | Slang: E, pills, brownies, Mitsubishi's, Rolex's, Dolphins, XTC<br>Appearance: usually in tablet form in all sorts of colours, some of which have pictures or logos stamped into them, or as powder<br>Taken: usually swallowed, although some people do smoke or snort them | 567,000 | 1.8 | £1-5 per pill | 48 |
| **Heroin** | A | Slang: brown, skag, H, horse, gear, smack<br>Appearance: comes as a white powder when it's pure. Owing to the range of substances it's cut with, street heroin can be anything from brownish white to brown<br>Taken: can either be smoked, dissolved in water and injected or snorted | 41,000* | 0.1 | £25-100 per gram | 713 (heroin and morphine) |
| **LSD** | A | Slang: acid, blotter, cheer, dots, drop, flash, hawk, L, lightening flash, liquid acid, Lucy, micro dot, paper mushrooms, rainbows, smilies, stars, tab, trips<br>Appearance: usually sold as tiny squares of paper with pictures on them, but it can be found as a liquid or as tiny pellets.<br>Taken: sucked and swallowed | 7,000 | 0.2 | £1-5 per tab | - |
| **Mushrooms** | A | Slang: liberties, magics, mushies, liberty cap, shrooms, Amani, agaric<br>Appearance: brown, dried-up mushrooms<br>Taken: often eaten raw or are dried out and stored | 201,000 | 0.6 | £6 per ounce, dried | - |
| **Amphetamines** | A/B | Slang: speed, Phet, Billy, Whizz, Sulph, Base, Paste, Dexies.<br>Appearance: off-white or pinkish powder or white pills<br>Taken: dabbed onto the gums, snorted, swallowed, mixed in drinks or injected | 421,000 | 1.3 | £8-12.50 per gram | 92 |
| **Cannabis** | B*** | Slang: black, blow, Bob Hope, dope, draw, ganja, grass, hash, hashish, hemp, herb, marijuana, pot, puff, resin, sinsemilla, skunk, soap, spliff, wacky backy, weed.<br>Appearance: hash is a blacky-brown lump made from the resin of the plant. Grass or weed is made from the dried leaves and looks like tightly packed dried herbs.<br>Taken: most people mix cannabis with tobacco and smoke it as a spliff or a joint. Some people put it in a pipe or bong, make tea with it or put it in food | 2,616,000 | 8.2 | £35-160 per ounce depending on type and quality | 17 |
| **Any drug** | | | 3,186,000 | 10.0 | | 2,570** |

* Figures for heroin and crack may be underestimates as types of groups that use these, e.g. people living in homeless hostels, tend not to overlap with crime survey respondents.

** Number of deaths where selected substances were mentioned on the death certificate. More than one drug may have been present so, for e.g. a death involving heroin where cannabis was also found will show up in both heroin and cannabis figures. Cocaine and crack are indistinguishable in the body after death so are not shown seperately. Total deaths includes anti-depressants and painkillers such as paracetamol.

*** Cannabis was reclassified from a Class B to Class C substance in 2004, but the Government have decided it will now be reclassified as Class B, effective from January 2009.

- None or no available data.

Data for England and Wales. Sources: 'Usage Estimates - British Crime Survey 2006-07', crown copyright. Average price - 'Drugs - facing facts', RSA Commission on Illegal Drugs, Communities and Public Policy. Deaths: Health Statistics Quarterly 36, ONS, crown copyright. More details: FRANK, www.talktofrank.com, crown copyright.

# Heavy cannabis use

## New report highlights impact of heavy cannabis use on vulnerable young people

Heavy cannabis use among vulnerable young people can exacerbate existing social problems, such as low educational achievement, homelessness and unemployment, according to a new report for the Joseph Rowntree Foundation (JRF) from the University of Bedfordshire. However, for others, particularly those in higher or further education, the effects appear to be relatively benign.

*The impact of heavy cannabis use on young people* drew on 100 interviews with 16- to 25-year-olds selected because they had been using cannabis on a daily basis for the past six months. Most were smoking 'skunk'.

When asked about the positive and negative consequences of taking the drug, the young people initially only listed what they felt to be positive: relaxation, socialising, and the feeling of being 'stoned'. It was only when various aspects of their lives were probed in more detail that associations between their use and problems such as unemployment, educational underachievement and homelessness became apparent – particularly for those with less structured lives. Moreover, those with the greatest number of social problems tended to use most heavily.

The report also found that some of the 30 professionals working with young people (such as youth workers and hostel workers) interviewed as part of this research saw cannabis as less harmful than the young people in the study did. This may be because of their differing experiences of cannabis use in previous decades, when high-strength herbal cannabis was less widely available. However, it raises questions about professionals' awareness of the potentially compounding effect of heavy cannabis use on the problems experienced by vulnerable or excluded young people – particularly if young people are unlikely to identify these problems themselves.

The report's author, Dr Margaret Melrose, said, 'Young people may not be aware of the extent to which cannabis use might exacerbate their existing social problems, and professionals who have had experience of cannabis users in the past may assume the effects are relatively harmless if they take young people's assessment of the impact of cannabis use in their lives at face value. More probing may be required in order to explore the level and nature of cannabis use and how this may be adding to a young person's problems.'

### Note

The full report, *The impact of heavy cannabis use on young people: vulnerability and youth transitions* by Margaret Melrose with Penny Turner, John Pitts and David Barrett is published by the Joseph Rowntree Foundation as part of the Drug and Alcohol series.
*24 October 2007*

⇨ The above press release is reprinted with kind permission from the Joseph Rowntree Foundation. Visit www.jrf.org.uk for more information.
*© Joseph Rowntree Foundation*

# Can ecstasy kill?

## Is ecstasy really the killer drug it was reported to be back in the '90s? Recent studies rank it safer to use than some legal drugs, so what's the story? TheSite.org sorts the fact from the fiction

### The latest findings

According to the Home Office there have been over 200 reported ecstasy-related deaths in the UK since 1996, however, other sources suggest that the drug is 'far safer than aspirin'. So what's the truth?

The 2008 BBC *Horizon* Programme *Is alcohol worse than ecstasy?* examined a call by experts to use modern knowledge to update the drug policies first put in place in 1971. 'Recent research has analysed the link between the harmful effects of drugs relative to their current classification by law... Perhaps most startling of all is that alcohol, solvents and tobacco (all unclassified drugs) are rated more dangerous than ecstasy, 4-MTA and LSD (all class A drugs),' the programme reported.

In fact, ecstasy ranked 18th in the list of 20 drugs, with one being most harmful. It came just above Poppers (19) and Khat (20), which are both legal and have not caused any known deaths.

### Is ecstasy safe?

There's evidently a lot of confusion about the safety of ecstasy, but do these findings mean that ecstasy is safe? According to Ruth Goldsmith, from the independent drug information and expertise centre DrugScope, the answer is no.

'Ecstasy can kill, and just because your mate is OK it doesn't guarantee that you will be. Over 200 otherwise healthy young people have died in the UK after using ecstasy since the 1990s.'

## Heatstroke and ecstasy

Most people who have died taking ecstasy experienced symptoms associated with severe heatstroke, because the drug messes with the mechanism that controls body heat. 'Experts believe that ecstasy-related deaths often result from the combined effects of the drug and the exertion of dancing for long periods in hot places, such as nightclubs or raves, rather than from any toxic effects of the drug,' explains Ruth.

According to the Home Office there have been over 200 reported ecstasy-related deaths in the UK since 1996, however, other sources suggest that the drug is 'far safer than aspirin'

Ecstasy stimulates the nervous system. In a club setting this can encourage users to dance for long periods of time, and if the place is hot and humid overheating problems can occur. If the body temperature exceeds 40 degrees there is a real risk of fatal respiratory collapse. MDMA, the active chemical in ecstasy, is believed to have some anti-coagulative properties (which means blood can't clot properly). Under such conditions, this can lead to internal and external bleeding in some people, and ultimately death.

Warning signs of heatstroke include:
⇨ Cramps in the limbs;
⇨ Fatigue and faintness;
⇨ Headaches and vomiting;
⇨ Inability to pee even if you feel the need, which is more severe than usual on ecstasy.

## Other dangers

Ecstasy raises blood pressure and heart rate. In some cases, this can put a fatal strain on users who have a pre-existing or undiagnosed heart condition.

## Reducing the risks

'No one can tell you how high the risks of taking ecstasy are, and the only way to completely reduce the risk is not to use the drug at all,' explains Ruth. 'Research shows that in 2006, 16 people died after having used ecstasy alone; and a further 26 died having used ecstasy with other drugs.

'It's estimated that around 567,000 people used ecstasy in 2006/07. While the number of people who died compared to those who used the drug may seem small, the risk certainly exists. Unfortunately, each time you take ecstasy, you're journeying into the unknown.'

If you are going to use ecstasy:
⇨ Do it with friends who know what you're taking and when you've taken it;
⇨ Clubbers can reduce the risk of overheating by replacing the fluid they've lost through sweating. Take regular breaks from the dancefloor, and sip at a pint of something non-alcoholic, like fruit juice, isotonic sports drinks or water every hour;
⇨ Don't drink too much fluid. It's believed that some victims misunderstood the importance of sipping a pint of non-alcoholic fluid every hour, and instead drank in excess. As ecstasy is thought to cause water retention in the body, especially in the brain cells, the resulting pressure can cause vital body functions to shut down. This was the cause of Leah Betts' high-profile death in 1995;

⇨ Don't mix your drugs – and that includes alcohol, which can increase your risk of dehydration, and any prescribed drugs you may be taking;
⇨ Don't drive while using drugs;
⇨ Don't buy drugs from people you don't know.

## Long-term health risks of ecstasy

The jury is still out on the long-term effects of ecstasy use. Some people believe that using ecstasy can cause depression in later life. 'We have not seen a significant body of evidence that supports this theory, but then again, most of those who were using ecstasy when it first became popular in the 1990s are only now reaching their late 30s and early 40s,' explains Ruth.

'Ecstasy affects the way the brain uses and produces chemicals such as the neurotransmitter serotonin, linked to feelings of pleasure. That's where the drug's mind-altering capacity comes from, but we don't know whether ecstasy users are putting themselves at risk of longer-term impacts on the brain's ability to manage serotonin production normally.'

With thanks to DrugScope for help compiling this article.
*Written by Susie Wild*

⇨ The above information is reprinted with kind permission from TheSite.org. Visit www.thesite.org for more information.

© TheSite.org

# Drug deaths

## How many people die from drugs?

The straight answer is that we do not know exactly how many drug-related deaths there are in the UK. This is because:

### Drug deaths

There is no one organisation that collects information about drug-related deaths, for all of the UK.

---

## There is no one definition of what we mean by drug-related deaths

---

There is no one definition of what we mean by drug-related deaths. For example, it could include:
⇨ people who are dependent on drugs and overdose;
⇨ suicides by overdose of people who have no previous history of using drugs;
⇨ accidental poisoning or overdose;
⇨ ecstasy-related deaths where people have died from overheating through dancing non-stop in hot clubs rather than from the direct effect of the drugs;
⇨ deaths associated with cigarette smoking;
⇨ deaths from accidents where people are drunk or under the influence of drugs;
⇨ murders and manslaughters where people are drunk or under the influence of drugs;
⇨ deaths from driving while drunk or intoxicated;
⇨ deaths from AIDS among injecting drug users;
⇨ deaths which had nothing to do with the presence of a drug in the body.

Cause of death is recorded on death certificates but doctors may not mention drugs, even where drugs might be involved.

Despite these difficulties there are estimates of the possible number of deaths associated with different drugs:

### Tobacco

It is estimated that each year in the UK around 114,000 people die from tobacco-related diseases, particularly from cancer, respiratory diseases and heart disease.

### Alcohol

Estimates of annual alcohol-related deaths in England and Wales vary from 5,000 to 40,000. This includes deaths from cirrhosis of the liver and other health problems from long-term drinking, deliberate and accidental overdose, traffic deaths, fatal accidents while drunk etc.

### Solvents

A national register of solvent-related deaths recorded 47 deaths associated with volatile substance abuse in 2004. This number shows a small decline from previous years with an average of 61 deaths for the years 1999-2004.

### Ecstasy

Deaths associated with different illegal drugs are also difficult to judge accurately. One exception is ecstasy with over 250 ecstasy-related deaths being reported between 1999 and 2004.

### AIDS

Deaths from AIDS among injecting drug users who have contracted HIV by sharing injecting equipment are also difficult to judge exactly. However, by December 2004 over 4,200 drug injectors had tested positive for HIV in the UK. Of that total over 1,200 [29%] had been diagnosed with full-blown AIDS and 1545 had died.

### Other drugs

In relation to the whole range of problems which can happen to those who use drugs, death is by far the least likely outcome, but one which, not surprisingly, attracts most attention and causes most concern. Like all data about illegal drug use, information about deaths comes from a variety of sources that combine to present a patchy and incomplete picture. Hence this is a highly simplified overview of what we know about deaths from drug use and how these compare to deaths caused by alcohol and tobacco.

### Sources of data

Data is held by the Office of National Statistics (ONS) and the General Register Offices (GRO) for Scotland and Northern Ireland. Data is also collected by the national programme on Substance Abuse Deaths (np-SAD), based within the International Centre for Drug Policy at St George's Hospital, University of London. It was set up initially to track and monitor the deaths of drug addicts who had been notified to the Home Office. St George's Hospital, University of London also collate the annual survey of solvent deaths.

ONS figures for drug-related deaths in England and Wales for 1993 was about 860 deaths rising to just over 1,420 in 2004. (In recent years an additional 220-280 drug-related deaths have been reported each year in Scotland.) These figures include accidental and deliberate overdose with medicines (excluding paracetamol which is related to roughly 1000 deaths a year. Most of which is suicide). However, the most recent statistics show that deaths involving drugs misuse have dropped to 1,427 in 2004 (from a figure of 1,666 in 2000) although the number of deaths involving specific drugs like cocaine and amphetamines (including ecstasy) have risen over the last 10 years.

With many of these deaths people had also been using other drugs and indeed may not have died if they had not been taking more than one drug.

⇨ The above information is reprinted with kind permission from DrugScope. Visit www.drugscope.org.uk for more information.

© DrugScope

# Types of drug-related death

## Information from the National Treatment Agency for Substance Misuse

Drug-related deaths are hard to define and to quantify. There is no one definition of what is meant by drug-related death. However, the NTA uses the definition set out by the Office of National Statistics (ONS), who produce national data on drug-related deaths:

*'Deaths where the underlying cause is poisoning, drug abuse, or drug dependence and where any of the substances are controlled under the Misuse of Drugs Act (1971).'*

(Office of National Statistics, ONS: 2006)

There are two broad categories of drug-related death:

**1. Sudden-onset deaths – typically associated with overdose**

Sudden-onset drug-related death is associated with overdose caused by opiate-based drugs (heroin or methadone), which are implicated in 70 per cent of cases. Often this type of mortality involves the use of opiates with other depressant drugs like alcohol and benzodiazepines.

The UK research evidence base clearly highlights who is most likely to die from an overdose and when that death is most likely to occur:

**Who?** This type of death is particularly noted amongst opiate drug users with a reduced tolerance.

**When?** Such opiate drug users are particularly vulnerable in the transitional periods of their drug using career. For instance when:

⇨ leaving prison;

⇨ discharged from drug treatment (especially 'unplanned' discharges);

⇨ leaving residential drug treatment (Tier 4).

**2. Gradual-onset deaths – associated with blood-borne viruses (BBV)**

Gradual-onset drug-related deaths occur from BBVs such as hepatitis C and B viruses and the Human Immunodeficiency Virus (HIV), which may lead to death many years after the first initial transmission of the infection.

There have been recent increases in the levels of BBVs amongst drug misusers (particularly those who inject). This increase is more marked in certain groups, including those injecting crack with heroin and homeless drug users. Worryingly, BBV incidence has also increased among new (predominantly younger) injectors and there has been a rise in the rate of sharing of injecting equipment.

⇨ The above information is reprinted with kind permission from the National Treatment Agency for Substance Misuse. Visit www.nta.nhs.uk for more information.

© *Crown copyright*

# Street drug trends

## DrugScope street drug trends survey 2007: two-tier cocaine market puts drug in reach of more users

DrugScope is today publishing the results of its *Druglink* magazine 2007 Street Drug Trends survey. Key trends uncovered by the survey indicate that the UK cocaine market is maturing and expanding with the drug as affordable as it has ever been. In many areas dealers are offering two grades of cocaine to buyers, effectively dividing their sales into 'economy' and 'luxury' cocaine, putting it in reach of more – and younger – users.

The survey compiles feedback from 80 drug services, drug action teams and police forces in 20 towns and cities across the UK and represents a snapshot view of current UK street drug trends.

The two-tier cocaine market sees dealers selling cheaper, more heavily cut cocaine to students, pub users and those on low incomes at around £30/gram, while targeting more affluent consumers with a higher quality drug at around £50/gram. Worryingly, some drug charities have confirmed that the age of clients coming forward with problems relating to cocaine use is dropping. Overall, official statistics show that cocaine use is relatively stable, but feedback from the survey indicates that use among young people may be growing.

In some areas young people are buying cheap, low-grade cocaine to mix with other drugs. Many police forces and drug services are seeing an increase in polydrug use with more young people using cocaine as well as alcohol, cannabis and ecstasy.

Over the last decade, cocaine's position in the UK drug economy has shifted significantly. Use of the drug is no longer restricted to the rich although it has not completely lost the glamorous associations of its past. Many users appear unconcerned by the drug's class A status and do not associate the drug with its serious health risks that include heart problems, mental ill health and the potential for dependency.

British Crime Survey statistics show a steep rise in cocaine use in the late 1990s with levels of use remaining relatively constant since 2000.

### Other drug trends

Other trends reflected in the survey include a similar two-tier market for ecstasy-type drugs. In some areas, the bottom has fallen out of the ecstasy pill market with the average street price of a pill now as low as £2.40, with pills most commonly sold in batches of 3

## Cocaine use among young people

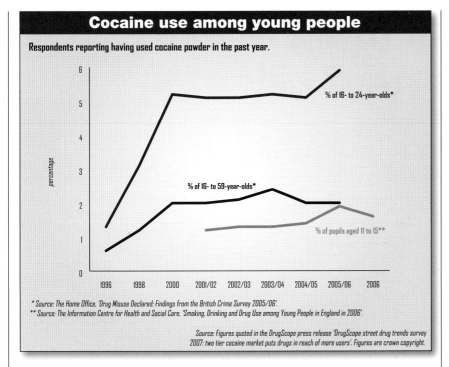

Respondents reporting having used cocaine powder in the past year.

% of 16- to 24-year-olds*

% of 16- to 59-year-olds*

% of pupils aged 11 to 15**

*percentage* (y-axis: 0, 1, 2, 3, 4, 5, 6)

(x-axis: 1996, 1998, 2000, 2001/02, 2002/03, 2003/04, 2004/05, 2005/06, 2006)

\* Source: The Home Office, 'Drug Misuse Declared: Findings from the British Crime Survey 2005/06'.
\*\* Source: The Information Centre for Health and Social Care, 'Smoking, Drinking and Drug Use among Young People in England in 2006'.

Source: Figures quoted in the DrugScope press release 'DrugScope street drug trends survey 2007: two tier cocaine market puts drugs in reach of more users'. Figures are crown copyright.

to 5 for £10. Pills sold as 'ecstasy' often contain no MDMA and are instead made from an amphetamine ('speed') base. In response more drug users are willing to pay a premium for crystal or powder MDMA at an average price of £38 per gram.

In Birmingham it has been reported that crystal and powder MDMA now take up 35 per cent of the market share (compared to 5 per cent ten years ago). The low MDMA content of most ecstasy pills in the area has seen teenagers as young as 15 turning to the hallucinogenic drug ketamine. Young people's drugs services in Birmingham have consequently stepped up their health messages around the use of ketamine.

Young people's use of alcohol as a replacement for illegal drugs when they are either not available or too expensive is of concern to several agencies.

Previous trends picked up by the *Druglink* Street Drugs survey – including the combined dealing and use of heroin and crack cocaine in speedballing, anabolic steroid misuse and the rarity of crystal meth – all remain significant in 2007. Apart from heroin, which has dropped in price by an average of £10 per gram since 2004, drug prices have remained relatively stable.

DrugScope's chief executive, Martin Barnes, today responded to the findings of this year's survey:

'We do not wish to exaggerate the extent of cocaine use but our survey does reveal some worrying trends. The use among young people, the drug's affordability and the combination with alcohol and other drugs is clearly a concern.

'There is little if any evidence that current efforts to tackle supply are impacting on the availability and price of cocaine, indeed dealers are able to meet the demands of different users by creating a two-tier market. One of the reasons why crystal meth remains relatively rare in the UK may be because there is such an established and profitable market for cocaine.

'DrugScope is aware that the Home Office is planning a campaign around cocaine use through FRANK, but remain concerned about the impact of this year's government funding cuts to young people's drug and alcohol services.

'The current drug strategy has focussed on breaking the links between drugs and crime with most resources dedicated to tackling the use of heroin and crack cocaine. We are concerned that we may be entering a new era of 'problem drug use' relating less to heroin and crack and more to the misuse of alcohol, cocaine, cannabis and ecstasy. The longer-term public health impacts of such a shift should not be underestimated.'
*13 September 2007*

⇨ The above information is reprinted with kind permission from DrugScope. Visit www.drugscope.org.uk for more information.
© *DrugScope*

## Street drug prices

Average UK national street drug prices

| Drug type | 2006 | 2007 |
|---|---|---|
| Herbal cannabis (standard quality) per ounce | £70.00 | £87.00 |
| Herbal cannabis (good quality) per ounce | £121.00 | £134.00 |
| Resin cannabis per ounce | £54.00 | £55.00 |
| Heroin per gram | £46.00 | £43.00 |
| Cocaine per gram | £43.00 | £43.00 |
| Ecstasy pill | £3.00 | £2.40 |
| Crystal/powder MDMA per gram | £40.00 | £38.00 |
| Amphetamine per gram | £9.70 | £9.80 |
| Ketamine per gram | £28.00 | £25.00 |

Source: 'DrugScope street drug trends survey 2007', DrugScope.

# Legal drug craze is new killer

*Once it was cocaine, speed or heroin, but now the fashion is for legal pills, washed down by spirits. Last week's news that actor Heath Ledger died from an overdose of prescription tablets shed light on a startling new trend – misuse of over-the-counter pills now kills more Americans than illegal drugs. Elizabeth Day in New York.*

Alex is a man who prides himself on sticking to routine. He likes to start the day with a large cappuccino from Starbucks and to end it with a handful of anti-depressants washed down with vodka. 'It's my treat after coming home from work,' he says. 'I guess it just chills me out a little.'

In many ways Alex, 31, is a typical well-heeled young New Yorker. He works in finance, holidays in the Hamptons and enjoys partying at the sort of exclusive nightclubs where having your name on the guest list is a prerequisite to entry. He also likes to get high on prescription drugs.

Tonight he is celebrating a friend's birthday at Marquee, one of the city's hippest nightspots. The main bar, lined with leather banquettes, is cast in a shadowy half-light. In the upstairs lavatory there is a small framed sign on the back of the door reminding guests the use of illegal drugs will not be permitted.

But Alex would not consider himself a drug abuser. For him, those small white Xanax tablets on his bathroom shelves are simply a recreational accompaniment to the $15 Grey Goose vodka martini he has just been served. And, what's more, they're entirely legal.

Over the past five years the United States has seen a ferocious increase in prescription drug abuse. According to the 2006 National Survey on Drug Use and Health, 49.8 million Americans over the age of 12 have reported non-medical use of illicit drugs in their lifetime, 20.3 per cent of the population. Among teenagers aged 12-17, prescription drugs are second only to marijuana in popularity, and in the past 15 years there has been a 140 per cent increase in painkiller abuse. It is the fastest-growing type of drug abuse in the US. Even more worryingly, prescription drugs have made it on to the party scene as a legal, seemingly safe, way to recreate an illicit high.

---

**Over the past five years the United States has seen a ferocious increase in prescription drug abuse**

---

Until last month this was a largely silent epidemic. But the death of Heath Ledger, a regular at Marquee and other nightclubs, thrust it into the spotlight. The 28-year-old actor died from 'acute intoxication' caused by an accidental overdose of anti-anxiety medication and prescription painkillers.

'Americans love to get pills for everything that ails them,' says Dr Howard Markel, a professor of paediatrics and psychiatry at the University of Michigan. 'The misuse of those drugs has become one of the major health problems of our time.' The UK has less of a prescription culture than the US, although many experts believe the advent of internet pharmacies means it is only a matter of time. In the US, where pharmaceuticals are advertised on prime-time television, pill-popping has become normalised, a socially acceptable means of alleviating stress, sleeplessness or anxiety.

The most commonly abused prescription medications fall into three categories: opiate-based painkillers (OxyContin and Percocet); central nervous system depressants prescribed for anxiety and sleep disorders (Valium and Xanax); and stimulants, used to treat attention deficit disorders (Ritalin and Adderall).

Within these categories, the pharmaceutical industry has provided a full set of substitutes for just about every illegal narcotic available. Methylphenidate, the active chemical in Ritalin, targets the brain's pleasure-producing centres in the same way as cocaine. Antidepressants can act as serotonin-boosting 'uppers'. A few years ago OxyContin, an extremely powerful painkiller developed for cancer patients, became known as 'hillbilly heroin' after an epidemic of abuse took root in poor rural communities.

Such mishandled drugs now kill 20,000 a year, nearly twice as many as 10 years ago.

Dependence on legal drugs is not a new problem – during the American Civil War morphine abuse was labelled 'the soldiers' disease' – but the practice of prescribing drugs has metamorphosed from a medical treatment of last resort to a way of life. 'The problem has been greatly worsened by the internet, and that affects all countries – including Britain,' says Susan Foster, of the National Centre on Addiction and Substance Abuse at Columbia University, New York. 'As long as you have a credit card, anyone can log on and have potentially lethal drugs delivered to their door. You don't even need a prescription. You have what's called an "online consultation" where you are asked how old you are, how bad your pain is.'

The substances most commonly traded over the internet are tran-quillisers such as diazepam and stimulants like Ritalin. However, the most dangerous are the opiates, which include codeine and morphine.

The painkiller fentanyl can act like heroin and traffickers get hold of supplies by forging stolen prescriptions, breaking into pharmacies and stealing stocks or buying the drugs from patients who have been prescribed it. Another opiate painkiller, buprenorphine – prescribed for heroin addicts trying to kick their habit – is peddled in countries as diverse as India, Iran, Finland and France. From 2001-05, the global consumption of buprenorphine more than tripled to 1.5 billion daily doses.

Doctors are woefully ignorant of the dangers; a 2005 study by Casa found that 43.3 per cent of them did not ask about drug abuse when taking histories. Even if they do, the seasoned drug abuser will go from one doctor to the next until they get the quantities they want – a practice known as 'doctor-shopping'.

This was Jeana Hutsell's experience. A petite 35-year-old from Canton, Ohio, with cropped peroxide blonde hair and square-framed glasses, Hutsell became hooked on Percocet, an opiate-based painkiller, when she was prescribed it 12 years ago after an operation for Crohn's disease. 'I went to the doctor with abdominal cramps and he began writing me copious prescriptions,' she says. Within a year, her habit had escalated to 60 pills a day and she was sewing emergency stashes

into the lining of her handbag. 'I felt they gave me personality. They made me chattier, friendlier.'

Hutsell began forging prescriptions, sometimes walking into hospital casualty departments over the weekend and saying she had run out. 'I felt justified and safe because my doctor was giving them to me. I wasn't getting them on the streets – I was going to a pharmacy.'

Now the fashion among recreational drug users is for legal pills, washed down by spirits

Whereas illegal street narcotics – heroin or crack cocaine – are more likely to be used by the poorer socio-economic classes, prescription drugs have become the preserve of the rich. In the privatised American healthcare industry, these pills do not come cheaply: an antidepressant like Wellbutrin can cost from $1,000 to $2,400 a year.

Wealthy individuals also enjoy the luxury of paying private physicians – known as 'script doctors' – to provide them with prescriptions. And often, because the drugs are viewed as performance-enhancers, they will be taken by those at the higher end of the social strata: by the college students and Wall Street traders. In the 1980s cocaine was the glamour yuppie drug. Now, the line of white powder is being

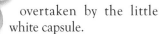

overtaken by the little white capsule.

Phoenix House is a tall, grey stone building on the Upper West Side, a former 19th-century hotel with mosaic-tiled floors in the hall. The genteel appearance belies its gritty purpose: Phoenix House is a rehabilitation centre for drug and alcohol abusers, treating 6,000 people a day. In recent years, such centres have seen a substantial increase in prescription drug admissions – some counsellors say that they account for 90 per cent of new patients.

Professor David Deitch, the chief clinical officer, does not want to use the word 'epidemic', but he concedes that 'the genie is out of the bottle'. 'You see prescription drug abuse in the same circles that you saw cocaine abuse – the high-performing executive class. They might have a big day, so they take some something to get to sleep. Then they'll take another pill the next morning to enhance their performance. Then they'll go out and use all kinds of drugs at a party, and then to recover from the party the next morning they'll take a different pill. It's pervasive.'

Celebrities who have admitted their own struggles with prescription medication include Elizabeth Taylor, the talkshow host Rush Limbaugh, and Cindy McCain, the wife of the Republican presidential candidate John McCain. More recently, there have been rumours that Britney Spears has been self-medicating. The impact has percolated down to impressionable adolescents. One of the most popular forms of recreation among high-school students is the 'pharm party'. Teenagers raid their parents' medicine cabinets, then pool their resources. 'You throw your drugs into a bowl in the middle of the room, then people pick pills out and

chase them with alcohol,' says Susan Foster. 'We've seen these internet recipe sites where you go online to find out how to mix drugs for a certain effect. You can trade drugs online – in fact, at one college the students reported that they had a prescription drug trade forum on the university website.'

Markel tells the story of one of his patients, a 16-year-old student called Mary, who liked to down a few tablets of OxyContin with a single shot of vodka. She called the combination 'the sorority girl's diet cocktail' because it gave a stronger kick of inebriation with fewer calories than alcohol alone.

'There's a cachet to this sort of drug abuse, encouraged by the Paris Hiltons and the Lindsay Lohans going into rehab, so it becomes a really cool druggy, party culture,' Markel says. 'Now teenagers don't want to smoke and drink, they want to take a pill because it's so easy to get and some of them can really make you feel good.'

But it is easy to overdose on prescription drugs, partly because your consciousness is impaired and it can be difficult to remember how many you've taken, and partly because mixing medication without specialised knowledge can produce fatally toxic results. And however legal these drugs might be, their misuse carries the same consequences as illegal narcotics: the familiar, dispiriting tale of the addict losing their family, friends, job, home and, sometimes, their life. After two years of Percocet addiction, Jeana Hutsell took stock of the wreckage her life had become: 'I was homeless, I didn't have a car, my family didn't like me. I realised that I was the cause of all my problems. That was the turning point.'

Others are not so lucky. Randy Colvin, an abuser of Valium, Xanax and Percocet, died of a drug overdose on his 35th birthday. 'We tried to save him and we lost,' says his older brother Rod. 'For 15 years we tried to get him into treatment and each time he would be in denial, he would be furious with us. My mother and I even tried to get a court order so that he could be sectioned. We did everything we possibly could. Addiction is a family disease. His death was very painful.'

For Heath Ledger's parents, the grieving process is still in the rawest stages. Their son cemented his fame for reasons that were nothing to do with his talent. Instead he is for ever associated with a seedy death on the floor of a Manhattan apartment, just one more victim of the pill-popping epidemic that has become America's secret illness.

### Danger zone
*Painkillers*
Popular brands include Nurofen and Solpadeine, which can prove addictive.
*Anti-anxiety drugs*
Tranquillisers have been involved in numerous recent fatal overdoses.
*Sleeping tablets*
Users can become dependent in just two weeks. Ledger was taking Restoril.
*Anti-depressants*
Prozac withdrawal symptoms are common and can be physically painful.

⇨ The following correction was printed in the Observer's For the record column, Sunday 17 February 2008. Above, we identified Xanax as an anti-depressant. Xanax is prescribed for generalised anxiety disorder, anxiety associated with depression and panic disorder, but it is not used for the treatment of depression.
*10 February 2008*
© *Guardian Newspapers Ltd 2008*

# Next year's drug

## Observations on addiction

### By Jeremy Sare

Experts on addiction, including senior police officers, are warning that we could be on the verge of an epidemic of a particularly grim drug, one that is highly addictive and can lead to psychosis, loss of teeth and an increased risk of heart disease and strokes.

You've seen the drug education posters showing the progressive decline of a pretty 20-year-old girl into a skull-faced fiend? This dramatic descent is typical of the effects of methamphetamine – or 'crystal meth', 'crank', or 'ice', to give it three of its street names.

Methamphetamine is an extraordinarily powerful stimulant that has had a devastating impact in North America, South Africa, Australia and south-east Asia. Often, it emerges in one social group, such as the gay community or biker gangs, but then its use spreads with bewildering pace.

Hamid Ghodse, president of the United Nations International Narcotics Control Board, is unequivocal on the subject. 'If I want to pick on one major drug problem pandemic today,' he says, 'it is methamphetamine.'

In Britain, only about 20 laboratories have been uncovered so far. However, the police think we may be on the cusp of an explosion in use. Detective Sergeant Andy Waite recently told Radio 5 Live: 'We are effectively at the point Australia was in 1998 . . . in four years it could be as big a problem here as crack cocaine.'

Meth is made from a cocktail of nasty, often toxic, chemicals (red phosphorus, iodine, ephedrine). It is 'cooked up' in kitchens and outhouses, often in poor, rural areas, forming into 'crystals' that are usually smoked in a pipe, although it can be injected or taken in pill form. Despite its grim origins, the 'high' appears to be like no other, a tremendous sense of superiority combined with an immense rush of euphoria.

Lee, a 42-year-old composer from New York, describes the effects. 'It gave me a sense of power. It made me feel sexual. It was like all the switches in my body and my brain felt like they finally got turned on.'

Unlike crack, the high does not diminish rapidly but is maintained for seven to ten hours. Users often stay awake for five days at a stretch, barely eating or drinking. It costs £50 a gram, about the same as heroin. Where methamphetamine use is rife, there is substantial addiction-related crime.

---

**We could be on the verge of an epidemic of a particularly grim drug, one that is highly addictive and can lead to psychosis, loss of teeth and an increased risk of heart disease and strokes**

---

John Marsden, of the Institute of Psychiatry, wrote the report on methamphetamine for the government's Advisory Council on the Misuse of Drugs. 'Meth has a very high dependence liability,' he says. 'After prolonged use, the euphoria disappears – there are many cases of stimulant psychosis revealed by anxiety, extreme paranoia and violence.'

Dr Marsden feels that the police are containing the problem but that the labs in Holland which supply much of Britain's Ecstasy could switch to methamphetamine production easily. If they did, Britain could be 'very vulnerable'.

The US has the biggest problem of any country. In 2006, there were an estimated 731,000 users, all prey to the serious social costs of methamphetamine use, including risky sexual behaviour. A recent rise in HIV/Aids among gay men in the US has been attributed to its use.

Unlike heroin, there is no effective substitute treatment for the drug. Relapse is common. Longer-term users often develop 'meth mouth' where their lips are covered in sores

and their teeth fall out. 'Meth kids' are easily spotted – they show the usual signs of parental neglect but also have burns on their feet because of corrosive chemicals left around by their addicted parents.

About half the users are women (only 30 per cent of heroin and cocaine users are female), many attracted by its weight-loss properties.

But Sebastian Saville, director of the drugs helpline Release, believes there is no reason yet to be too worried: 'Release has had very few calls from meth users. Ecstasy is still very cheap here so there isn't a gap in the market. Often meth use in other countries takes off in rural areas where there is limited access to Ecstasy, heroin or coke. In Britain, people can get most drugs anywhere.'

So, should we be worried? The chemicals and instructions for manufacturing crystal meth are easily obtained from the internet. Drug problems in the US have in the past always crossed the Atlantic. In the mid-1980s, there was a huge increase in crack in the US, whose police authorities warned Britain to be ready for the same. For a while, it didn't happen. The government now estimates we have nearly 60,000 crack users.

John Reid, when home secretary, reclassified crystal meth from B to A in January 2007, and regulations controlling the precursors used to make the drug have been strengthened. But there is no government programme

warning of the dangers of meth, although the Home Office drug advice website gives some information.

A Home Office spokesperson says: 'The latest evidence from the Association of Chief Police Officers [Acpo] shows that the current prevalence of methamphetamine remains low, but we take this issue seriously and are not complacent.

'Acpo continues to monitor the extent of methamphetamine in the UK and we are working with them to ensure that we have an appropriate response as the intelligence and evidence develops. In addition, we are already taking a number of preventative steps as part of our efforts to tackle drug use and associated crime.'

But even if the government appears alive to the issues, it risks finding itself largely helpless in the face of a huge increase in the use of this deadly drug.

A report at the end of last month from the drug dependency charity AddAction calculated that Britain's Class A drug addiction problem costs the nation around £16.4bn a year, more than one and a half times the cost of holding the Olympic Games in 2012.

*28 February 2008*

⇨ The above information is reprinted with kind permission from the *New Statesman*. Visit www.newstatesman. com for more information.

# Rise in ketamine use among young people

## Monthly use among clubbers trebles in 10 years

Use of the illegal drug ketamine is increasing among young people worldwide, particularly within the electronic dance music scene, according to new research.

Academics at the Universities of Bath and Lancaster in the UK see the findings as evidence of a 'continued desire for altered states of intoxication by at least some groups within society' despite the 'persistence of prohibition'. Ketamine was recently classified as a Class C substance in the UK – its use was not illegal until 1 January 2006.

Dr Fiona Measham of Lancaster University said: 'Ketamine has come out of nowhere. Ten to fifteen years ago, few people were choosing to take ketamine but now it's in the "top 7" drugs according to Drugscope. Over the past 10 years it's gone from 2 to 3 per cent of clubbers to three times that in terms of monthly usage.'

A user in one of the studies on ketamine, 'Carl', described it as 'the most fun you can have for twenty quid'.

Dr Karenza Moore of Lancaster University said: 'Since classification British users report little or no change in price, availability, patterns of use, nor their perceptions of ketamine, leading us to question the deterrent value of current British drug policy.'

This adds to growing concern amongst experts over the UK government's drug policy, particularly its persistent belief in the deterrent value of the ABC classification system, evident in recent moves to reclassify cannabis to Class B.

In addition, the academics criticise the UK government for criminalising ketamine use without providing harm minimisation information of relevance to young party-goers, particularly given the dangers associated with using ketamine in combination with alcohol.

Their research is the focus of a special issue of the journal *Addiction Research and Theory* on ketamine use in the UK, Europe and the US. Published this week, it will be the first international collection of papers of its kind.

---

**Use of the illegal drug ketamine is increasing among young people worldwide, particularly within the electronic dance music scene**

---

Ketamine was originally developed in the 1960s as an anaesthetic and is still used by the veterinary and medical professions. However, it is also taken recreationally. Whilst usage in the general population remains low, indications are that ketamine use is increasing amongst young people from all socio-economic backgrounds: including students, those in full-time employment, young professionals and particular cultural groups such as clubbers and members of the free party scene.

Both cheap and easily available, ketamine is thought to be enjoyed by young people due to its short-lasting, mildly hallucinogenic properties. Users regard ketamine as safer and more easily controlled than LSD, 'magic' mushrooms or other hallucinogenic drugs; and cheaper and more fun but less addictive than cocaine.

Users usually consume ketamine by snorting lines of the white powder into the nasal passage to be absorbed by mucous membranes in a similar manner to cocaine. First-time ketamine use by some of those interviewed was due to mistakenly thinking they had been offered cocaine powder rather than ketamine powder, leading to confusion and, in a minority of cases, distress.

Researchers found ketamine is increasingly popular among older and more experienced recreational drug users who tend towards polydrug use: taking more than one drug either consecutively or concurrently with other drugs such as ecstasy, cocaine and cannabis for their combined effects. For many users ketamine is part of these 'weekend polydrug repertoires' during a night out, with ecstasy and cocaine taken in clubs and ketamine use favoured alongside cannabis in post-club settings.

Despite the hedonism associated with such weekend polydrug use, researchers found ketamine was usually consumed in a relatively safe and sensible manner, in small quantities on an occasional basis, at chill-out parties after leaving dance clubs, where users felt more able to control the environment and reduce the likelihood of negative experiences.

Amongst women, however, there was

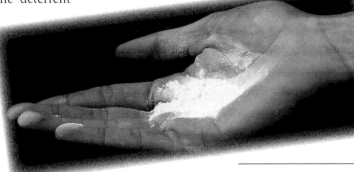

concern that taking ketamine might make some women more vulnerable than when under the influence of other popular illicit drugs such as ecstasy and cocaine.

Within the British free party scene, the effects of ketamine were seen to diminish the collective and communal experiences of dance events, enhanced by ecstasy. For some non-users of ketamine, there was irritation or resentment at people taking ketamine in public social settings then needing to be 'looked after', due to their intoxicated state.

Increased ketamine use is also evident in the USA and Hong Kong. In Hong Kong ketamine has replaced ecstasy as the most popular illicit drug to be consumed in clubs.

Edited by academics from Bath and Lancaster Universities, this international and multidisciplinary collection of papers is devoted to the social and cultural uses of ketamine. Based on seven studies in the UK, the USA and Hong Kong, combining criminological, sociological and psychological research with contemporary cultural analysis and first-hand accounts, it is believed to be the most comprehensive overview of ketamine use to date.

Overall, the seven studies included in the special issue highlight the diversity of practices and meanings about ketamine – both in terms of how it is consumed and the kinds of groups that consume it.

The editors are Professor Christine Griffin (University of Bath), Dr Fiona Measham (Lancaster University), Dr Karenza Moore (Lancaster University), Dr Yvette Morey (University of Bath) and Dr Sarah Riley (University of Bath).
*12 May 2008*

⇨ The above information is reprinted with kind permission from the University of Bath. Visit www.bath.ac.uk for more information.
*© University of Bath*

# Enslaved by K

**A whole new realm of the imagination opened up when David Eggins took his first line of ketamine. In the real world, however, he was lucky to get out alive ...**

**By David Eggins**

I first took ketamine in 2002, between my second and third years at university. I was mourning the end of a long-term relationship with a massive bender. It was a weekday afternoon and I was necking ecstasy and playing pool when a mate asked me if I'd ever tried 'K'.

**K – which was originally developed as an anaesthetic and is still used to treat animals and occasionally humans – did wonders for my ego**

We didn't even finish the game. We went back to my flat and it was love at first snort.

One of the problems with K is trying to explain what a 'K-hole' is like. Nothing can prepare you for the chaos. All you can say is that it is really weird, but until you have taken it, even the most drug-fried mind can't comprehend what 'weird' can mean. Most people hate it; it's just too much. Many are sick because of a sort of mental travel sickness. But I didn't throw up: I adored it.

The K-hole has been described as an endless dimension to explore, and that's exactly what it is. Space, time and language either have no meaning or become ridiculously distorted. It can seem as if you are travelling through time or seeing into the future, as if you are living multiple lives or not living at all. And you feel something coming, something huge with you at the centre, because there is a massive messiah complex in there as well.

I have been at one with the cosmos, communicated with the universal forces that are our true gods, and been told that death should be embraced as the next level of everything. All complete bollocks, of course, but I never got that from a wrap of coke.

For a little while I had my ketamine use under control and found it therapeutic.

K – which was originally developed as an anaesthetic and is still used to treat animals and occasionally humans – did wonders for my ego. I lost my sense of shame and fear of death, I felt liberated. I got an unexpected first at uni, I was writing book reviews for a national magazine, and I had a new, beautiful girlfriend. I hung out with fellow K-heads, or 'wrong 'uns', as we were known to other druggies, whose company I loved. I felt part of something and life was good, but all the time I was using more and more K.

It is the tolerance that gets you. When you start, a gram might see you through three or four nights out. Before long it will be enough for only a few hours and, sooner or later, you start using it at home. I started selling it to pay for my habit.

Today, ketamine is a class-C drug, on a level with cannabis, but until a few years ago it was regulated only by the Medicines Act, and although it was still illegal to deal in it, the police took less of an interest. I used to buy it in liquid form and then cook it in a pan or microwave to create powder. The liquid came from India, often disguised as rose water. Someone would have it posted to their house and I would buy a litre from them for £300. That litre would turn into 50 grams, which I sold for £15 or £20 a gram. It never felt like a risk, at least as far as the police were concerned. But

I couldn't have that much K around me without doing it, all the time.

If I wasn't at work – I had become a chef after leaving university – I was taking K.

I would take a gram during the break in my split shift. I would get home and sniff three grams in front of the television, and then take another three to bed with me. I had a line before work, not knowing if I had slept. And I was starting to get ill. I have always liked drink and drugs but, other than tobacco, I had never been truly addicted to anything before. I never used heroin or crack, and could tell when any substance was becoming a problem. I usually just got bored of something and moved on – but not this time. K may not be physically addictive, but it is compulsively psychologically addictive.

I stopped dealing when my girlfriend asked me to, hoping that this would help, but I was too far gone. I still did as much, but I started to hide it from her.

After about two years of using ketamine, I was spending more and more time in the toilet, and urinating was beginning to hurt.

I developed a stoop because my penis was always burning. One day, on a train, I had my first cramp attack; I thought my lung had collapsed. I went to a doctor, who told me to stop taking K or I would die, but then an older user told me not to worry, it was 'just K cramps'. He said that they wouldn't kill me, but I might wish that they would. Apparently they could last for days.

I still didn't stop. The cramps got worse, the blood and mucus began to appear frequently in my urine and I had to pee every 20 minutes. I lied more than I told the truth, particularly to my girlfriend, and I hated myself. I couldn't stand to be around myself and wanted to cause myself harm. K worked on both fronts.

I stopped going out because my friends didn't want to see me like that, I quit my job because I was in too much pain to work, and I lost the review gig because I could no longer read a book. I fell further into debt.

By the time I realised that ketamine was ruining my life, I no longer cared. I didn't want to die as such; I just

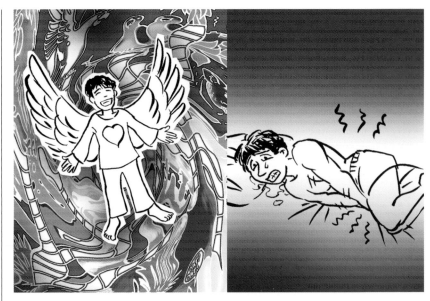

didn't mind if I did. My girlfriend couldn't save me. She begged me to leave the west-country town where I was living, surrounded by other K-heads, and move back to Devon, where I had grown up.

I told her I would, but I was lying. I didn't want to give up. I was positive I was going to die whether I did or not.

One evening, about a year ago, when I was supposed to be watching a friend's band play at our local, I found myself naked, writhing on my kitchen floor, racked with abdominal cramps and self-loathing, and praying.

Praying to a God I don't believe in to show Himself, to intervene, to give me something to believe in other than ketamine, and the certainty that my life was over. He didn't, but when the pain subsided, the relief was almost like a drug in itself.

In the end change was forced on me. A local street gang had tried to break into my flat on several occasions. They held a knife to my flatmate's throat as he left for work. We managed to fight them off, but I could hardly walk by then and weighed nine stone. It was the street or home. I called my mum.

Once back home, I could barely sleep and suffered from night terrors and sleep paralysis. I started to smoke cannabis, scored black-market codeine and Valium. And I kept begging my K dealers to send me some. I offered them silly money, but they still said no, because they truly were worried about me. Later, when I did find another source of K, I used

the bare minimum to get me through the craving.

So here I am, living on my mum's settee. I've got my health back but lost everything else, including my girlfriend. She had lost all trust, and in the end she realised she would be glad to see the back of me.

Do I think that ketamine should be higher than its class-C listing? No, but people should know what they are dealing with. By the time I did, it was too late. There is so much media coverage of illegal drugs, yet K is rarely mentioned, although it is everywhere and spreading fast. Most people who try it won't develop any major problems, but a minority of users get very sick. A friend of mine lost so much control over his bladder that he had to have a catheter fitted when he was 21, and there are going to be a lot more cases like this. He didn't know it was addictive either.

The one bright spot in all this is that the human body has amazing powers of recovery. If there is any addict of any substance reading this who thinks that they have destroyed their body beyond hope, you might be surprised what happens if you give it a break. Within a month of moving home, I got a job as a builder. I even pee like a normal person. Do I drink too much and smoke too much pot now? Yep. Do I still crave K when I'm down or depressed? Sometimes. Do I ever give in to those temptations? Never. Am I still a liar? Of course not, darlin', I promise.

*21 April 2008*

# Cost of UK's illegal drug habit hits £110bn

## Information from AddAction

**addaction**

The costs of illegal drug use in the UK have risen to £110bn over the past ten years according to new estimates published today. The staggering sum, which totals the health and crime costs of Class A drug use, would more than pay for the NHS for an entire year, claims a report by Addaction, Britain's biggest specialist drug and alcohol treatment charity.

Coming as the government prepares to unveil its new ten-year plan on drugs, the report highlights the savings made to the economy by drug treatment, but reveals that just three per cent of total spending on tackling drug-related behaviour in the past ten years went to tackling drug addiction in the UK. The current budget for drug treatment is set to fall by 10 per cent over the next three years.

Since the government's ten-year drug strategy began in 1998 the cost of drug-related crime has climbed to £100bn, with health costs contributing a further £10bn. Last year alone these costs came to £16.4bn, with each person remaining dependent on illegal drugs costing the country around £44,000 per year.

As well as damaging families and communities, the report outlines how drug addiction results in a huge loss of opportunity, not just to the individual but the economy as a whole. While the UK taxpayer currently spends just over £800m a year supporting drug users in benefits, getting 100,000 problem drug users back into work could generate as much as £2.3bn a year in additional taxes to the economy and disposable income.

Deborah Cameron, Addaction Chief Executive, said:

'Illegal drug use is costing the UK taxpayer £16.4 billion a year, which is more than one and a half times the cost of holding the Olympic Games in 2012.

> **'Illegal drug use is costing the UK taxpayer £16.4 billion a year, which is more than one and a half times the cost of holding the Olympic Games in 2012'**

'Many of the millions spent by the government on dealing with the consequences of the illegal drugs trade could be recovered if drug users were given a better route out of a life dependent on drugs. We have to ensure drug users get help but also a roof over their head and the chance of a job or training.'

Among other findings highlighted in the report:

⇨ Last year the total cost of providing medical care to Class A drug users was £560m.

⇨ The direct costs of processing all problem drug users through the criminal justice system comes to £2.6bn a year.

⇨ Drug-related deaths from Class A drugs cost £923m a year through loss of opportunity costs.

*25 February 2008*

⇨ The above information is reprinted with kind permission from AddAction. Visit www.addaction.org.uk for more information.

*© AddAction*

# New plan to tackle illegal drugs

## The plan calls for earlier intervention to get drug-using families into treatment, legal rights for police to seize property purchased with drug money, and new approaches to drug treatment

The government's new ten-year strategy for fighting illegal drugs is designed to ensure that fewer young people ever use drugs, and that those who do use drugs get help to kick the habit and re-establish their lives.

It aims to cut drug-related crime, and to reduce the damage that drugs do in our communities.

This year the government will invest almost £1 billion in the programmes behind the new strategy. This investment will help to:

⇨ extend police powers to seize drug dealers' assets, ensuring that crime doesn't pay;

⇨ place a more responsibility on drug-users on benefits to get treatment and jobs;

⇨ tackle drugs through neighbourhood policing;

⇨ strengthen and extend international agreements to intercept drugs before they reach the UK;

⇨ focus on families where parents use drugs; and prioritising treatment for parents in order to protect children;

⇨ try new approaches that allow more flexible use of resources, and more personalised treatment;

⇨ increase the use of community sentences, including some that require drug rehabilitation;

⇨ develop support for drug treatment, so that those who quit drugs get training and support so they can get back to work, and re-establishing their lives.

### Drug use at 11-year low

Over the last decade, use of illegal drugs in the UK has fallen to an 11-year low. Drug-related crime has dropped by a fifth over the last five years.

Our unprecedented investment in drug treatment has more than doubled the number of people getting treatment – 195,000 in the last year.

Compulsory drug testing of people who have been arrested, backed up by tough punishment – including prison sentences – has contributed to a fall in recorded acquisitive crime.

But tackling drugs remains a formidable social problem. Use of Class A drugs costs the UK £15 billion a year in crime and health costs alone.

### Use of illegal drugs 'destroys families'

Home Secretary Jacqui Smith said the strategy well help to reach the government's goal of ensuring that fewer people use drugs.

'Illegal drug use is unacceptable. It wastes lives, destroys families and damages communities,' she said. 'We want those who do use drugs to enter and finish treatment, and move on to lead healthy, drug-free lives.'

She said the government plans to continue to send a clear message that it is on the side of communities.

'We demand respect for the law, and we will not tolerate illegal or anti-social behaviour. But we will provide help for those who are trying to turn their lives around, to get off drugs and into work. However, we expect drug users themselves to take responsibility, and we will help them to do so.'

### Tailored approach

Among other things, the government will alter the rules of the benefits system in order to provide a more personalised approach. This will ensure that drug users receive support tailored to their needs.

In return, they will be required to attend drug treatment sessions.

The plan aims to strike the right balance between personal responsibility and governmental support.

So known drug users receiving benefits will be required – as a first step – to attend an assessment for drug treatment.

Health Secretary Alan Johnson pointed out that gains have already been made in terms of treatment, and over the past ten years treatment options have exponentially expanded. More people are getting treatment and they're waiting less time for help.

'Every drug user is different,' he said. 'This strategy ensures that treatment is personalised to suit

individual needs. A key element is an innovative new pilot scheme which will help drug users who are on benefits get into treatment, get a job and live a drug-free life.'

### Faster treatment for families with drug problems

Children, Schools and Families Secretary Ed Balls said only a small minority of parents are drug users, but even a small number is too many as the situation puts children at risk.

Because of that concern, the new strategy ensures that parents with dependent children will get better and faster access to specialist drug treatment.

'At the heart of the new drugs strategy is recognising the influence of families in tackling the problem,' he said. 'So we will help parents by providing more information and support to help them talk to their children about drugs.'
*27 February 2008*

⇨ The above information is reprinted with kind permission from the Home Office. Visit http://drugs.homeoffice.gov.uk for more information.

© *Crown copyright*

# The new drugs strategy explained

**The government today published its report, *Drugs: Protecting Families and Communities*. Senior political correspondent Andrew Sparrow summarises its key points**

### The problem

⇨ There are an estimated 332,000 problem drug users in England.
⇨ Class A drug use costs the country £15.4bn a year in crime and health costs.

---

**24% of people aged 16 to 24 have used an illegal drug in the past year**

---

⇨ Between a third and a half of theft and burglary is estimated to be drug-related.
⇨ 24% of people aged 16 to 24 have used an illegal drug in the past year.
⇨ 10% of people aged 16 to 59 have used an illegal drug in the past year.
⇨ The UK illegal drug market is estimated to be worth between £4bn and £6.6bn a year.

### Crime measures

⇨ Police to have the power to seize cash and assets belonging to suspected drug dealers on arrest, rather than on conviction. 'Those who buy "bling", plasma screens and other household goods, to avoid circulating cash, will have their assets seized before they have a chance to disperse them.'

⇨ A greater range of goods will be subject to the asset recovery programme, which enables convicted drug dealers to have their assets seized. The 12-year time limit governing asset recovery will also be abandoned.
⇨ Asset seizure agreements to be negotiated with other countries, starting with the United Arab Emirates in April 2008, 'so dealers can't channel proceeds abroad'.
⇨ Antisocial behaviour orders to be imposed on drug dealers after conviction. These could ban them from entering certain areas, or engaging in certain behaviour linked to drug dealing.
⇨ Further drug screening at airports.
⇨ Police to be encouraged to make greater use of the powers they have to close crack houses.
⇨ Wider use of drug intervention programmes, which involves offenders having to take treatment programmes.

### Benefit measures

⇨ Drug users to be threatened with benefit cuts if they do not participate in drug treatment programmes. 'We do not think it is right for the taxpayer to help sustain drug habits when individuals could be getting treatment to overcome barriers to employment.'
⇨ Increasing support available to drug users to help them get housing and work.

LIVERPOOL JOHN MOORES UNIVERSITY LEARNING SERVICES

➪ Trial projects to 'explore the potential of a more flexible use of funding to address individual needs'.

### Drug treatment services

➪ Programmes involving prescription of injectable heroin and methadone to addicts who do not respond to other forms of treatment to be rolled out, 'subject to the findings, due in 2009, of pilots exploring the use of this type of treatment'.

➪ 'New and innovative treatment approaches' to be investigated.

➪ Programmes using 'positive reinforcement techniques' to be piloted.

---

### The UK illegal drug market is estimated to be worth between £4bn and £6.6bn a year

---

➪ Addicts to be encouraged to make wider use of mutual aid support networks.

➪ Prison drug treatment programmes to be improved.

### Support for families

➪ Family members such as grandparents who take on caring responsibilities in the place of drug-using parents to get additional support through a programme in which councils can pay those caring for children classified as 'in need'.

➪ More support for parents with drug problems so that children do not fall into 'excessive or inappropriate caring roles'.

➪ More family-based treatment services to protect young people.

### Drugs education

➪ Improved information and guidance to be available to all parents.

➪ Schools and colleges to be encouraged to see what they can do to identify and support.

➪ Further action to be taken to reduce underage sales of alcohol and cigarettes.

*27 February 2008*

# Tackling substance misuse – progress

---

### Facts and figures

➪ For every £1 spent on drug treatment there is a saving of £9.50 to society as a whole.

➪ The Government is investing £604 million in drug treatment in 2008/09.

➪ £54.3 million of new funding is being invested to expand inpatient detoxification and residential rehabilitation services.

➪ 195,000 people received treatment in 2006/07, 130% more than in 1998.

➪ Three out of four people stay in treatment for at least 12 weeks. (Staying in treatment for 12 weeks has a lasting positive impact and is a measure of successful treatment.)

➪ 96% of drug users are receiving treatment within three weeks of being assessed.

➪ Drug-related deaths have fallen by 13% since 2001 following sharp increases in the 1990s.

➪ Drug-related crime has reduced by 20% since 2003 among those individuals referred for drug treatment through the Criminal Justice System.

➪ 83% of young people are aware of FRANK, the government's drugs awareness campaign. The number of 15- to 18-year-olds agreeing that smoking cannabis damages the mind went up from 45% to 61% as a result of this campaign.

*9 July 2008*

➪ The above information is reprinted with kind permission from the Department of Health. Visit www.dh.gov.uk for more information.

# Drug use worldwide

## Key data from UN World Drug Report 2008

Following are figures and observations on global illicit drug production and use from the World Drug Report 2008 released on Thursday by the UN Office on Drugs and Crime (UNODC).

### World drug use

There were an estimated 165.5 million users of cannabis products (4 per cent of the world's population between the ages of 15 and 64), compared with 24.7 million users of amphetamines, 16 million users of cocaine, 12 million users of heroin and 9 million users of the psychedelic methamphetamine drug known as ecstasy.

Approximately 208 million people or 4.9 per cent of people aged 15 to 64 have used drugs at least once in the last 12 months.

### Opium/heroin market trends

In 2007, the opium/heroin market continued to expand due to cultivation increases in Afghanistan, which pushed up the area under opium poppy cultivation worldwide by 17 per cent. However, cultivation increased by 22 per cent in south east Asia, driven by a 29-per cent rise in Myanmar. This was south-east Asia's first increase in six years.

Afghanistan produced 92 per cent of the world's opium last year. Myanmar was the No. 2 producer.

### Coca cultivation

In 2007, the total area under coca cultivation in Bolivia, Colombia and Peru increased 16 per cent to 181,600 hectares (448,700 acres). This jump was driven mainly by a 27-per cent increase in Colombia.

Despite these recent increases, the global area under coca cultivation continues to be lower than in the 1990s and 18 per cent below the level recorded in 2000, 221,300 hectares (546,800 acres). Colombia continued to grow most of the coca.

Global cocaine production has remained stable over the last few years, reaching 994 metric tonnes in 2007, almost the same as in 2006 (984 metric tonnes). The majority of this amount – 600 tonnes in 2007 – came from Colombia.

Cocaine use has fallen in North America but is rising in Europe.

### Cannabis

Cannabis, mostly in the form of marijuana and hashish, continues to dominate the world's illicit drug markets in terms of pervasiveness of cultivation, volume of production and number of consumers. Global cannabis leaf production is estimated to have stabilised at around 41,400 metric tonnes in 2006. There was a 27-per cent decline in global cannabis seizures between 2004 and 2006.

Most was produced in North America in 2006 (55 per cent). The consumer market for cannabis products dwarfs those for the other drug groups.

*26 June 2008*

© *Reuters*

# Drug use in Europe

## Information from the EMCDDA

Note that these estimates relate to the adult population and are the most recent estimates available. For complete data and full methodological notes see the 2007 statistical bulletin.

### Cannabis

⇨ Lifetime prevalence: at least 70 million, or one in five European adults.
⇨ Last year use: about 23 million European adults or one-third of lifetime users.
⇨ Use in the past 30 days: over 13 million Europeans.
⇨ Country variation in last year use: 1.0% to 11.2%.

### Cocaine

⇨ Lifetime prevalence: at least 12 million, or around 4% of European adults.
⇨ Last year use: 4.5 million European adults or one-third of lifetime users.
⇨ Use in the past 30 days: around 2 million.
⇨ Country variation in last year use: 0.1% to 3%.

### Ecstasy

⇨ Lifetime prevalence: about 9.5 million European adults (3% of European adults).
⇨ Last year use: 3 million or one-third of lifetime users.

⇨ Use in the past 30 days: more than 1 million.
⇨ Country variation in last year use: 0.2% to 3.5%.

### Amphetamines

⇨ Lifetime prevalence: almost 11 million or around 3.5% of European adults.
⇨ Last year use: 2 million, one-fifth of lifetime users.
⇨ Use in the past 30 days: less than 1 million.
⇨ Country variation in last year use: 0.0% to 1.3%.

### Opioids

⇨ Problem opioids use: between one and eight cases per 1,000 adult population (aged 15–64).
⇨ Over 7,500 acute drug deaths, with opioids being found in around 70% of them (2004 data).
⇨ Principal drug in about 50% of all drug treatment requests.
⇨ More than 585 000 opioid users received substitution treatment in 2005.

⇨ Information taken from *The state of the drugs problem in Europe: annual report 2007*, and reprinted with permission from the EMCDDA. Visit www.emcdda.europa.eu for more.

© *European Monitoring Centre for Drugs and Drug Addiction*

# Young people and drug use

**Statistics from the survey *Drug use, smoking and drinking among young people in England in 2007***

This survey is the latest in a series designed to monitor smoking, drinking and drug use among secondary school pupils aged 11 to 15. Information was obtained from 7,831 pupils in 273 schools throughout England in the autumn term of 2007.

---

### In 2007, 17% of pupils said they had taken drugs in the last year and 10% in the last month

---

The prevalence of drug use has declined overall since 2001. For example, in 2007, 25% of pupils said they had tried drugs at least once, down from 29% in 2001. There were corresponding falls over the same period in the proportions of pupils who said they had taken drugs in the last year and the last month. The decline in the prevalence of drug use reflects a fall in the proportions of pupils who have ever been offered drugs over a similar period, from 42% to 36%.

In 2007, 17% of pupils said they had taken drugs in the last year and 10% in the last month. The prevalence of drug use is similar among boys and girls, and increases with age. 6% of 11-year-olds had taken drugs in the last year, and 3% in the last month; at the age of 15, 31% of pupils had taken drugs in the last year and 17% in the last month. There are slight differences between ethnic groups. Pupils of mixed and Asian ethnicity are more likely than white pupils to have taken drugs in the last month, though this difference is not seen for drug use in the last year.

As in previous years, pupils are more likely to take cannabis than any other drug; in 2007, 9% of pupils reported taking cannabis within the last year, a proportion which has fallen from 13% in 2001. Sniffing glue, gas, aerosols or solvents is the next most common form of drug use (6% of pupils in the last year), followed by sniffing poppers (5%). The use of other drugs by this age group is rare. Overall, 4% of pupils report having taken one of the eight Class A drugs asked about, though no single Class A drug had been taken by more than 2% of pupils in the last year. Two-fifths of pupils (39%) who took drugs in the last year took more than one type of drug.

Most pupils who take drugs do not do so often. A third (34%) of pupils who had taken drugs in the last year said they usually take drugs once a month or more, only 5% of pupils overall. Among those who had taken drugs in the last year, 28% said they had only ever taken drugs once, and a further 31% had taken drugs on five or fewer occasions.

The pattern of drug use varies according to what type of drugs pupils have taken. For example, pupils who have sniffed glue, gas, aerosols or solvents tend to be younger than pupils who have taken

other drugs, and there is evidence that much volatile substance use is experimental. Pupils' first drug use is more likely to be sniffing volatile substances than any other type of drug. Pupils who have taken volatile substances only are more likely than other drug users to say they have only tried drugs once and are less likely to report frequent drug use. A significant minority of pupils whose first drug use was sniffing volatile substances found them at school or home, and most did not feel noticeably different after trying them. This is unlike the experience of those who tried other drugs first; they were more likely to have got the drugs from friends and to have felt some effects – good or bad – as a result of their use.

In contrast, Class A drug use is more common among older pupils. The majority of those who report taking any Class A drugs – for example, cocaine, magic mushrooms, ecstasy or crack – say they take drugs at least once a month, and relatively few have taken drugs only once. Pupils who take Class A drugs are more likely than other drug users to report that they felt good as a result of taking drugs, and are less likely than others to say that they would like to stop taking drugs. At the same time, Class A drug users are much more

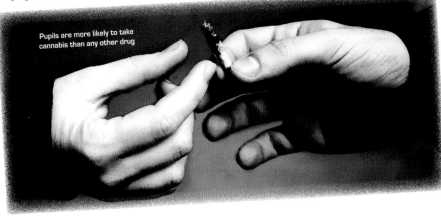

Pupils are more likely to take cannabis than any other drug

likely than other drug users to have felt that they needed treatment for their drug use.

As can be expected, there are some differences between pupils' first experience of drug use and subsequent drug taking. Pupils are more likely to try sniffing volatile substances than other drugs; 44% reported trying volatile substances only at the age they first tried drugs, compared with 25% who had taken cannabis only. Nearly three-quarters (72%) of pupils get their first drugs from friends. The most common reason for trying drugs is 'to see what it was like' (55%); relatively few pupils try drugs to get high or feel good (18%) or because their friends are taking drugs (17%). The first experience of drug taking is equally likely to leave the pupil feeling good (43%) or no different (44%). Pupils who remember their first experience of drug taking as good are most likely to go on to take drugs again.

Pupils who had taken drugs more than once were most likely to have taken cannabis only on the most recent occasion; 45%, compared with 21% who said they had sniffed glue, gas, aerosols or solvents only and 18% who had taken a Class A drug. Again, these drugs are most likely to have come from friends (74%). The reasons why these pupils are taking drugs are likely to have changed somewhat from the reasons for trying them. 43% of pupils said they took drugs most recently to get high or feel good. Though a significant minority (29%) still take drugs to see what it is like, or because their friends are doing it (17%), an increased proportion (21%) give 'I had nothing better to do' as their reason for taking drugs on the most recent occasion. Pupils who have taken drugs more than once are more likely than not to report a good experience on the most recent occasion (63%).

Pupils tend to feel that drug use is not acceptable behaviour within their age group. A minority think that it is OK for someone of their age to try cannabis once (10%), to try sniffing glue (9%) or to try cocaine (3%). They are even less likely to be sympathetic to regular drug use; 6% think it is OK for someone of their age to take cannabis once a week, 4%

to sniff glue once a week and 2% to take cocaine once a week. Attitudes change with age, in line with the prevalence of drug use; for example, 13% of 15-year-olds think that it is OK for someone of their age to take cannabis once a week, compared with 1% of 11-year-olds. Pupils also tend to feel that their parents would (or do) disapprove strongly of drug taking. Most (86%) think their families would try to stop them taking drugs, with smaller proportions thinking their families would try to persuade them to stop (13%), would do nothing (1%) or would encourage them (less than 1%).

Drug taking is associated with other hazardous behaviours; the odds of having taken drugs in the last year and in the last month increase with the frequency of smoking and the amount of alcohol drunk in the last week. Pupils who have been excluded from school or who have played truant also have a greater likelihood of having

taken drugs. The approach pupils' families take is also associated with whether or not they have taken drugs. The more lenient pupils perceive their families to be about drug taking, the greater the odds are that they will have taken drugs within the last year and within the last month.

The report also includes information findings on pupils' awareness of individual drugs, drug use among vulnerable pupils, whether and why pupils refuse drugs, beliefs about drug use among their peers, and teaching and other school policies concerning drug use.
*17 July 2008*

⇨ The above information is an extract from the report 'Drug use, smoking and drinking among young people in England in 2007' and is reprinted with kind permission from the NHS Information Centre. Visit www.ic.nhs.uk for more information.
*© Crown copyright*

# Primary school kids able to name illegal drugs

**Most primary school children are able to name at least four illegal drugs, a new study has shown**

The research conducted by Life Education consisted of surveys of 1,500 children between the ages of nine and 11 in schools in England and Northern Ireland.

Students were asked about the names of illicit drugs they were aware of as well as the reasons for taking the illegal substances.

The poll revealed that cocaine was the most well-known drug with over 71 per cent of children knowing of it. The next most well-known drug was cannabis with 64 per cent of primary school students having heard of it.

Other findings of the poll showed that 20 per cent of respondents felt that Class A drug cocaine was legal while 38 per cent cited the pressure to look cool as the main reason for using drugs.

A spokesman for the charity, Stephen Burgess, said: 'It is no use pretending that children under 11 don't know about drugs.

'These results show that they do and in order for them to approach the potentially challenging period of adolescence knowing the full facts rather than responding to hearsay and peer pressure, we need to reach children early – at primary school,' he added.
*21 June 2008*

⇨ The above information is reprinted with kind permission from politics.co.uk. Visit www.politics.co.uk for more information.
*© politics.co.uk*

# Dealing with drugs in the schoolyard

## Has the pill-pusher replaced the tuck shop? Christopher Middleton finds out

*money*

Once upon a time, children at private school used to blow all their pocket money at the tuck shop. These days, though, spare parental cash can end up being spent on cannabis rather than Curly Wurlys.

These dangers have been highlighted in a recently published book, *Mum, Can You Lend Me Twenty Quid?* (Piatkus, £14.99). In it, mother and teacher Elizabeth Burton-Phillips tells how her twin sons started taking soft drugs while at an independent school, then progressed to ecstasy, crack cocaine and heroine, until one of her boys, Nick, hanged himself at the age of 27.

The story has sent shivers through the private sector. But what should parents do when their children let on that fellow pupils at school take drugs? The first step, it seems, is to get to know the enemy.

'The drugs scene is completely different to what it was 20 or 30 years ago,' says Dr Pat Spungin of the parental website www.raisingkids. co.uk. 'If parents are going to have any credibility, they need to acquaint themselves with what's out there.'

Fortunately, this doesn't involve trawling dance clubs. Instead, the information can be found on the Drugscope website (www.drugscope. org.uk).

Here you can learn that 2CB (also known as Nexus and Spectrum) is a new, hallucinogenic variation on ecstasy and that Poppers (alias Rush and Locker Room) are liquid nitrites that you breathe in for a quick high and, although not actually illegal, can make you nauseous.

---

### 'The drugs scene is completely different to what it was 20 or 30 years ago'

---

So is now the time to panic? No, says Pat Langham, headteacher of Wakefield Girls' High School and president of the 200-strong, independent-sector Girls' Schools Association. 'You should be encouraged by the fact your child has chosen to open up to you,' she says. 'You will discourage them from ever confiding in you again if you immediately start delivering lectures, demanding names and threatening to tell the school.'

Certainly, barging into the head's office and denouncing the guilty pupils may not be the best course of action. Apart from the fact that your children may have got it wrong, there are issues of self-preservation involved. Not yours, but theirs.

'You've got to think of the consequences for your children,' says an adviser at Talk To Frank, the independent drugs advice line. 'If people find out it was your kids who talked, it could be dangerous for them.'

Good point. Especially if the school operates a zero-tolerance drugs policy, along the lines of one-puff-and-you're-expelled.

'If there's no chink of light, no second chance, it makes it more likely that people won't come forward with information and that the problem will remain in the shadows,' says Mark Pyper, head of Gordonstoun.

He scrapped the school's zero-tolerance policy on his arrival, 17 years ago, and feels that his aim to minimise drug abuse, and move towards eradicating it, has been more effectively achieved as a result.

One alternative, if you don't want to disclose specific details to the school, is to cloak your allegations in a degree of fogginess. At Gordonstoun, the head boy and head girl are asked to 'steer' staff in the general direction of miscreants (e.g. 'There's a problem in Year 10 Boys'). Alternatively, parents can get their offspring to ring Childline, which will inform the school but never breathe your name.

Before passing on any kind of tip-off, though, it's essential to look at the school's stated drugs policy to see what fate awaits the children you're pointing the finger at. Dr Martin Stephen, High Master of St Paul's School in London, thinks parents are more likely to divulge a drugs problem if they feel it will lead not to blind retribution but to rehabilitation.

At St Paul's, as at Gordonstoun, erring pupils are allowed to stay on at the school on three conditions: that they haven't been taking hard drugs; that they haven't brought those drugs on to school premises; and that they agree to a one-last-chance programme of random drug-testing.

'I loathe cannabis and believe it to be a lethal drug,' says Dr Stephen. 'That said, to operate a one-strike-and-you're-out policy is to deny the nature of childhood. You also tend to find that parents are 100 per cent in favour of a zero-tolerance policy until it's their child who's caught.

'As for children in the private sector being more vulnerable to drugs, I don't agree. I feel immense sorrow for Elizabeth Burton-Phillips and for her loss but, in my experience, drugs are just as prevalent in the State sector as in independent schools. None of us should be complacent.'

## Act now
*Ask for advice*
Contact Parentline Plus (0808 800 2222; www.parentlineplus.org.uk), or see the parental website www. raisingkids.co.uk.
*Wise up*
Research what drugs are out there in the Drugsearch section of the Drugscope website (www.drugscope. org.uk; 020 7940 7500).
*Ring Frank*
Get non-judgemental facts from people who know the drugs scene through the Talk To Frank helpline (0800 776600; www.talktofrank.com).
*Protect your child*
Rather than naming individuals, think about raising general concerns with the school. Alternatively, get your son or daughter to ring Childline (0800 1111), which will inform the school without disclosing your child's identity.
*13 October 2007*

# Gender differences in drug use

## Why girls are far more likely to abuse drugs like speed, Ecstasy and cocaine than boys. Information from The Scotsman

### By Shân Ross

Teenage girls are being exposed to drugs earlier than boys and experimenting with a wider range of narcotics from a younger age, a new survey has revealed.

The report by a leading youth drugs agency found girls and young women are more likely than boys to have taken almost every recreational drug, including Ecstasy, cocaine, LSD and amphetamines.

A quarter of females questioned admitted taking speed and Ecstasy, almost a half had used cannabis and more than one in five had tried cocaine. Ten per cent had taken the dance drug ketamine, 18 per cent had tried hallucinogenic mushrooms and more than 55 per cent had smoked.

The figures for males were lower, with about 15 per cent admitting to taking amphetamines, Ecstasy, cocaine and magic mushrooms, 6.9 per cent trying ketamine, 45 per cent using cannabis and less than a third smoking.

Researchers said the difference could be explained by girls and young women being exposed to drugs culture from an earlier age, both through older boyfriends and from being allowed into nightclubs.

It was claimed door staff are likely to 'turn a blind eye' to under-age girls who are heavily made-up and dressed for clubbing, especially if they were in groups or accompanied by an older boyfriend.

The annual survey by Crew 2000, an Edinburgh-based drugs advice centre, which looked at 18 drugs, found two-thirds of girls had accessed more drugs than males. The findings supported those of the latest Scottish Schools Adolescent Lifestyle and Substance Use Survey report in 2006 which found girls were accessing drugs in clubs and discos more than boys.

Carla Ellis, the project's operation manager, said:

'Girls mature at an earlier age and are subjected to a range of role models from celebrities like Kate Moss to other adult influences around them in everyday life.

'They are likely to have boyfriends who are a couple of years older and are able to get into clubs where they can access drugs. They reach a stage, earlier than boys, where they want to be mature and be accepted as part of that older group. Peer pressure can have an incredibly powerful effect on girls, contributing to the feeling that nothing can happen to them. Behaving as they do is a way of sticking two fingers up at society.'

Graeme Walker, 20, a PR and media student at Queen Margaret University in Edinburgh, said: 'You are more likely to see under-age girls in clubs where they can get speed,

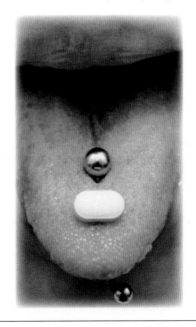

Ecstasy and coke. I still get [asked for identification] on the door because bouncers are more likely to check a boy's ID than a girl's. But, at the same time, they will let in an under-age girl in a low-cut top with no questions.'

Rowdy Yates, senior research fellow in Scottish Addiction Studies at the University of Stirling, added:

'One of the areas I've studied is heroin, and the majority of women have tended to become involved through older boyfriends and will continue that for many years.'

### I sold drugs to look cool, says Robina, 15

Robina was 15 and a pupil at an Edinburgh school when she met her 17-year-old boyfriend William at a party two years ago. His elder brother and friends introduced her to drugs and she ended up selling them to other pupils to appear 'cool'.

'I really enjoyed being part of that crowd,' she said. 'I'd never tried cannabis before and it made me feel part of things. It was all a scene – going to clubs to see bands.

'William's brother knew how to get stuff and that's the way I should have left it.

'I started showing off, making out I had contacts. Friends asked me to get them drugs and I ended up buying more for myself and selling it on.

'I definitely felt paranoid and was bad-tempered with my parents. Part of it could have been the drugs but I was stressed thinking I'd get caught on CCTV somehow. I wasn't remotely a drug dealer ... being silly got me into a mess.'

*12 April 2008*

© The Scotsman

# Supply of cannabis

## Cannabis supply to young people mostly through social networks

Cannabis supply to young people is largely through social networks and friendship groups rather than through overtly criminal drug markets. This is according to a new study from the Institute for Criminal Policy Research published by the Joseph Rowntree Foundation.

Just over 2.5 million young people (16-24) in England and Wales have used cannabis with an average starting age of 14. Yet how young people access and use the drug has rarely been considered in the UK. Scant research has been conducted into how the criminal justice or education systems deal with young people caught supplying or brokering cannabis – helping others access the drug but not for profit.

The report – *Cannabis Supply and Young People: 'It's a social thing'* – provides a snapshot of how young people in a large city and rural villages obtain cannabis. Researchers found that nearly all of the 182 young cannabis users interviewed were introduced to the drug by friends; used the drug with friends; and accessed the drug through friends. Only 6% had bought the drug from an unknown seller so most of them were insulated or distanced from overtly criminal drug markets.

Nearly all interviewees reported cannabis to be 'very easy' or 'fairly easy' to buy. Over three-quarters stated that they could acquire cannabis in less than an hour. 'Chipping in' and sharing cannabis with friends to make it more affordable was a common way of purchasing the drug for 70% of those interviewed. Of the sample, 45% reported involvement in cannabis transactions but they did not generally perceive themselves as dealers. Some, however, conceded that they could be seen as such by others. Most of the young people were aware that they would be arrested if they were caught selling cannabis and over three-quarters knew that there was no difference in sanctions between social and commercial supply.

Over half had taken cannabis into their school or college and slightly less than half had used cannabis there at some point. However, only a minority did this on a regular basis and the report authors found that the use of cannabis in school was unusual. While school drug policies they examined were often found to be consistent with national guidelines, sanctions for drug incidences varied across different schools.

Amongst those interviewed, 45% had either sold cannabis or brokered access to the drug without making a profit – nearly always to friends and acquaintances. They did not generally perceive themselves as dealers although they conceded that they could be seen as such by others and by the criminal justice system.

Professor Mike Hough, Director of the Institute of Criminal Policy Research, said: 'While the public stereotype of the drug dealer may be of an adult stranger "pushing" drugs to young people, in the case of cannabis, this is very rarely the case. Most young people get their cannabis from other young people – often without a profit being made.'

### Notes

**1** The full report, *Cannabis supply and young people: 'It's a social thing'*, by Martin Duffy, Nadine Schafer, Ross Coomber, Lauren O'Connell and Paul J. Turnbull is published by the Joseph Rowntree Foundation as part of the Drug and Alcohol series.

**2** A four-page summary (published in 2007) is also available.

**3** The study was based on interviews with 182 young people aged between 11 and 19. To participate in the research young people had to fit one of two criteria: that they had used cannabis on at least one occasion in the three months prior to interview and/or had brokered access or sold cannabis within the six months prior to interview.

*31 January 2008*

⇨ The above press release is reprinted with kind permission from the Joseph Rowntree Foundation. Visit www.jrf.org.uk for more information.

© Joseph Rowntree Foundation

# Drugs and politics

### Information from politics.co.uk

### What are drugs?

Drugs include a broad range of substances ranging from prescription medicines, to illegal street drugs such as cocaine and ecstasy, to readily available products such as tobacco and alcohol.

In public health and political terms, 'drugs' usually refers to recreational drugs, specifically those which are illegal under the Misuse of Drugs Act. Although technically a mind-altering substance, alcohol is not commonly included in the drugs debate, with binge drinking treated as a separate issue. Similarly, tobacco warrants its own debate.

### Background

The UK government has adopted a prohibitive stance towards recreational drugs, which is enforced through the Misuse of Drugs Act 1971. Prior to this act, drugs policy in the UK was relatively liberal but was reformed under pressure from the US, who pushed for the global criminalisation of drugs.

This makes it an offence to possess drugs for personal use or with intent to supply, or to allow premises you occupy or manage to be used for drug taking. It does not make it a specific offence to be under the influence of controlled substances.

The act created the Advisory Council on the Misuse of Drugs, which became responsible for distinguishing three separate classes of controlled substances, referred to as Class A, Class B and Class C drugs. This classification system both attempts to rank the harm caused by various drugs and set appropriate penalties for their use.

⇨ Class A: Punishable with up to seven years in prison or an unlimited fine or both for possession. Life in prison or unlimited fine or both for intent to supply. Includes; Ecstasy, LSD, cocaine, crack, magic mushrooms and amphetamines (if injected).

⇨ Class B: Punishable with up to five years in prison or an unlimited fine or both for possession. 14 years in prison or an unlimited fine or both for intent to supply. Includes: amphetamines, Ritalin and pholocodine.

⇨ Class C: Punishable with two years in prison, an unlimited fine or both for possession. 14 years in prison, or an unlimited fine or both with intent to supply. Includes' cannabis, tranquillisers, some painkillers, GHB and ketamine.

When assessing the classification of new drugs, the Advisory Council on the Misuse of Drugs hears evidence from law enforcement agencies, charities, professional bodies and scientific evidence. It classifies drugs using a risk assessment matrix, which covers nine types of term divided between physical harm, dependence and social harms.

---

**It has been argued that criminalising all drugs by definition creates a criminal subculture to meet demand for recreational substances**

---

### Controversy

Drugs policy in the UK falls under the domain of the Home Office. This places it as a criminal matter and yet many argue drugs policy would be better overseen by the Department of Health. Similarly, the ABC drugs classification system has been criticised for combining physical and social harm caused with criminal penalties.

The UK adopts a policy of prohibition towards drugs. Police constable Richard Brunstrom argues this has proved as effective as America's attempt to ban alcohol during the 1920s. There is a body of thought that argues drugs policy should shift from abstinence education and government attempts to disrupt supply to harm reduction policies.

Small-scale versions of this approach tend to target existing addicts and focus on teaching people to avoid overdose, needle exchanges and opioid substitutes.

It has also been argued that criminalising all drugs by definition creates a criminal subculture to meet demand for recreational substances. This in turn has been linked to other forms of crimes including gang violence. However, calls to legalise all drugs are politically unpopular and the late Mo Mowlam is one of the few members of the political establishment to have made the case for legalising all hard drugs.

The ABC system for classifying drugs has come under intense criticism, both from within parliament and the scientific community.

Numerous sources have accused the ABC system of inconsistency, noting that the criminal penalties ascribed to various drugs do not always equate to the harm caused. Richard Brunstrom has said the ABC system 'defies logic' and has no basis for excluding alcohol and tobacco.

A study published in the *Lancet* in spring 2007 concluded UK drugs policy was not fit for purpose. Looking at the harm caused by various narcotic substances, it found alcohol was the fifth most dangerous drug available, following heroin, cocaine, barbiturates and methadone, yet it is not included in the ABC system. Tobacco emerged as the ninth most dangerous drug, ahead of cannabis and the Class A drugs ecstasy and LSD.

The decision to include or reclassify a drug in the ABC system is invariably met with further controversy. Rising expectation in 2006 that crystal meth was set to surge in popularity in the UK led many to argue it should be reclassified as a Class A drug, underscoring the harm caused by the amphetamine. However, concerns were raised the resultant publicity from reclassifying the drug would draw attention to its effects and inadvertently increase its use. Nevertheless, in January 2007, crystal meth was reclassified as a Class A drug.

The reclassification of cannabis has provoked similar controversy. In 2004 it was revised downwards from a Class B to a Class C drug after it was argued this would give police more time to concentrate on 'hard' drug users. In practice this means it is unlikely an adult caught in possession of cannabis will be arrested and charged. Instead they will likely receive a warning and have the drug confiscated, unless certain conditions apply.

---

## The ABC system for classifying drugs has come under intense criticism, both from within parliament and the scientific community

---

A selection of anti-drug campaigners, scientists and MPs have argued the reclassification of cannabis was inappropriate and ignored the evidence that stronger strains of 'skunk' cause more harm than the cannabis available during the 1960s and 1970s. In summer 2007 Gordon Brown indicated he is prepared to reclassify cannabis as a Class B drug and the issue will be considered as part of a wide-ranging consultation on drugs policy.

### Statistics

⇨ For every £1 spent on drugs treatment, £9.50 is saved in drug-related crime and health costs.

⇨ Around four million people have at least one illicit drug use each year and around one million young people use Class A drugs at least once a year.

⇨ Ten per cent of 16- to 59-year-olds admitted using drugs in the past year, placing drug use at its lowest level for ten years.

⇨ Number of deaths with heroin use listed on the death certificate in 2005: 842.

⇨ Number of deaths with alcohol listed on the death certificate in 2005: 6,627.

*Statistic 1: (Source: Department of Health 2007); statistic 2: (Source: Home Office 2007); statistic 3: (British Crime Survey 2006-07); statistics 4 & 5: (Source: Office for National Statistics)*

### Quotes

'The current classification of controlled drugs has no sound underpinning logic. Most importantly the ABC system illogically excludes both alcohol and tobacco. Drugs and psychotropic substances are simply not going to go away as if by magic.'
*Police constable Richard Brunstrom, October 2007.*

'I did break the law... I was wrong... drugs are wrong,'
*Home secretary Jacqui Smith, July 2007.*

*14 November 2007*

⇨ The above information is reprinted with kind permission from politics.co.uk. Visit www.politics.co.uk for more information.

© *politics.co.uk*

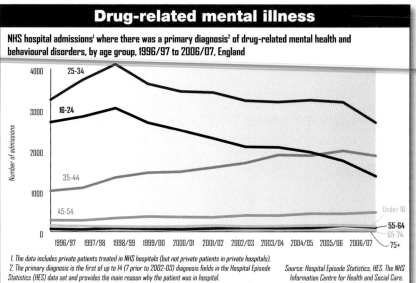

**Drug-related mental illness**

NHS hospital admissions[1] where there was a primary diagnosis[2] of drug-related mental health and behavioural disorders, by age group, 1996/97 to 2006/07, England

1. The data includes private patients treated in NHS hospitals (but not private patients in private hospitals).
2. The primary diagnosis is the first of up to 14 (7 prior to 2002-03) diagnosis fields in the Hospital Episode Statistics (HES) data set and provides the main reason why the patient was in hospital.

Source: Hospital Episode Statistics, HES. The NHS Information Centre for Health and Social Care.

# Drug legislation

## Summary of the main UK drug-related legislation

### Misuse of Drugs Act 1971

Controls the unauthorised use of drugs deemed capable of 'having harmful effects sufficient to constitute a social problem'. Defines the offences relating to production, cultivation, supply and possession of nearly all drugs with abuse and/or dependence liability. Of particular relevance to employers is the offence committed by the occupier of premises if he/she knowingly permits the production or supply of any controlled drugs, the smoking of cannabis or certain other activities to take place on the premises.

### Medicines Act 1968

Governs the manufacture and supply of medicines, some of which are also controlled by the Misuse of Drugs Act.

### Customs & Excise Management Act 1979

Penalises unauthorised import and export of illegal drugs. Customs and Excise use compounding proceedings which mean, in essence, that the offender is allowed to pay a fixed penalty in lieu of prosecution.

The Home Office limits the use of compounding in drugs cases to offences involving herbal cannabis or resin not exceeding a total weight of 10 grammes. Although details of compounding proceedings are not generally made public, details may be disclosed to an employer if; the nature of the offender's job helped him to commit the offence, or the offender's job required a particularly high degree of unimpaired faculties or judgement.

### Drug Trafficking Act 1986

Makes it an offence to sell articles for the administration or preparation of illegal drugs, and allows for the seizure of assets related to the proceeds of drug trafficking.

### Controlled Drugs (Penalties) Act 1985

Increased the maximum penalties for trafficking in Class 'A' drugs.

### Intoxicating Substances (Supply) Act 1985

Controls sales and supply of solvents to under-18s in the UK.

### Road Traffic Act 1972

Makes it an offence to be in charge of a motor vehicle whilst unfit to drive through drink or drugs (including solvents).

### The Health & Safety at Work Act 1974

Section 2 of the Act requires that employers ensure, as far as it is reasonably practicable, the health, safety and welfare at work of their employees. Section 7 of the Act requires employees to take reasonable care of the health and safety of themselves and others who may be affected by their acts or omissions at work. It is possible that in certain circumstances charges may be brought against an employer who knowingly allows a drug abuser to continue working without doing anything either to help the abuser or to protect the rest of the workforce.

⇨ The above information is reprinted with kind permission from Parents Against Drug Abuse. Visit www.pada.org.uk for more information.

*© PADA*

# Using harm to classify drugs

## Information from the Medical Research Council

**A** new study published today in the *Lancet* proposes that drugs should be classified by the amount of harm that they do, rather than the current A, B, and C divisions used in the UK Misuse of Drugs Act.

The new scientifically-based ranking places alcohol and tobacco amongst the most damaging of substances. These socially accepted drugs were judged to be more harmful than cannabis, and more dangerous than the Class A drugs LSD and ecstasy.

Harmful drugs are currently regulated according to classification systems that are meant to reflect the harms and risks of each drug. The scientists argue that these are generally neither specified nor transparent, which reduces confidence in their accuracy and undermines health education messages.

Professor David Nutt from the University of Bristol, Professor Colin Blakemore, Chief Executive of the Medical Research Council, and colleagues, identified three main factors that together determine the harm associated with any drug that could potentially be abused: Physical harm to the individual user caused by the drug; the tendency of the drug to induce dependence; and the effect of drug use on families, communities, and society.

Twenty drugs were then scored by an expert panel. The scores in each category were combined to create an overall estimate of harm and a ranking in the classification.

To provide familiar benchmarks for comparison five legal drugs, alcohol, khat, solvents, poppers and tobacco, were scored. Ketamine, a drug that has since been classified, was included in the assessment.

The process provided roughly similar scores for drug harm when used by two separate groups of experts.

Lead author Professor David Nutt said:

'Drug misuse and abuse are major health problems. Our methodology offers a systematic framework and process that could be used by national and international regulatory bodies to assess the harm of current and future drugs of abuse.'

Professor Colin Blakemore added: 'Drug policy is primarily aimed at reducing the harm to individual users, their families and society. But at present there is no rational, evidence-based method for assessing the harm of drugs. We have tried to develop such a method. We hope that policy makers will note the resulting ranking of drugs differs substantially from their classification in the Misuse of Drugs Act and that alcohol and tobacco are judged more harmful than many illegal substances.'

Original paper: 'Development of a rational scale to assess the harm of drugs of potential misuse' published in the *Lancet* volume 369.
23 March 2007

⇨ The above information is reprinted with kind permission from the Medical Research Council. Visit www.mrc.ac.uk for more information.
© *Medical Research Council*

# Q&A: cannabis reclassification

### Why is cannabis in the news?
The Home Office has defied the opinion of its own medical advisers by announcing that cannabis will be upgraded to class B again. The Advisory Council on the Misuse of Drugs published the findings of a review of the drug's classification today, which concluded that cannabis should remain class C.

### What did the review look at?
Gordon Brown ordered the review in response to concerns among doctors and MPs that the current classification of cannabis did not reflect the danger it poses to users' health. Several studies carried out since the drug was downgraded from class B in 2004 have warned that it damages users' mental health.

### What are the health concerns?
There is particular concern about skunk, a potent form of cannabis linked to mental health disorders. In 2005, 10,000 11- to 17-year-olds were treated for cannabis use – 10 times the number a decade ago.

Cannabis plants are increasingly cultivated at home and include high levels of the active ingredient of cannabis, THC – delta-9-tetra-hydrocannabinol – which encourages addiction and can cause symptoms including short-term memory loss and anxiety and panic attacks.

### By David Batty

Between 1975 and 1989, government records show cannabis resin contained between 6% and 10% THC, with cannabis leaves – or herbal cannabis – lower at 4-6%. However, more recent figures from the Forensic Science Service show that while resin has remained of similar potency, homegrown herbal cannabis has doubled in strength to 12-14% THC.

During their review of the drug's classification, the advisory council was told that the incidence of new schizophrenia cases reported to GPs had gone down, not up, between 1998 and 2005, indicating a weak link between increased potency and use in the past two decades and mental health problems.

A 2006 report by the council found sufficient scientific evidence to suggest a causal link between cannabis use and long-term psychotic symptoms, but said the risks from using the drug were not serious enough to warrant reinstating it to class B.

Cannabis has also been linked to other medical complications, including ectopic pregnancies and miscarriages.

### Are the mental health worries justified?
What is not clear from the research is whether the psychotic symptoms linked to cannabis use are only short-term or whether they may persist after use of the drug has ceased.

In 2005, a Danish study found that almost half the patients treated for cannabis-related mental disorder went on to develop schizophrenia. The mental health charity Mind found the

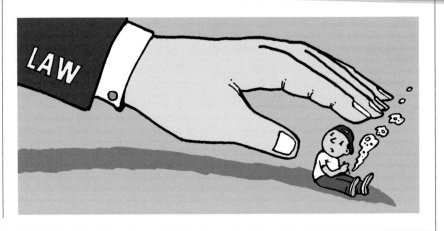

number of people taken to hospital with psychotic episodes had risen since cannabis was downgraded to class C. A study in the *British Medical Journal* in 2004 found that while there was a slight risk of psychotic symptoms among young cannabis users, the drug had a much stronger effect on those who already had mental health problems.

An authoritative summary of research into the effects of cannabis on psychosis was published in the *Lancet* last year. It concluded that smoking cannabis increased the risk of schizophrenia by at least 40%. The research analysed previous data on the effects of the drug on tens of thousands of people, indicating that there are at least 800 people suffering serious psychosis in the UK after smoking cannabis. But the study offered little more in the way of understanding the impact that more potent strains are having. This is partly because of the ethical problems in conducting long-term trials to compare regular cannabis with skunk.

The advisory council was apparently persuaded to recommend retaining the drug's class C status after examining the findings of a new study by Keele University. The study, expected to be published later this year, found no evidence that rising cannabis use in the 1970s, 1980s and early 1990s had led to increases in the incidence of schizophrenia later on.

Research by the DrugScope charity also suggested the growth in homegrown skunk had been overstated because less potent varieties were more easily cultivated. Mental health campaigners point out that although the health risks are significant, reported use has also fallen since the classification of cannabis was downgraded.

According to the British Crime Survey, 21.4% of 16-24-year-olds had used cannabis in 2005-06, compared with 28.2% in 1998-99.

### How would reclassification affect cannabis users?

If cannabis were again made a class B drug, it would carry more severe penalties for possession. The maximum penalty for being found in possession of a class C drug is two years in prison plus an unlimited fine; for class B drugs it is five years in jail plus an unlimited fine.

The maximum penalty for supplying or dealing class C drugs and B drugs is the same – 14 years' imprisonment plus an unlimited fine.

The Association of Chief Police Officers said it would not adopt a tougher approach towards the simple possession of cannabis if ministers upgraded the drug to class B again. Instead, they would retain the basic approach of not making an arrest and taking the offender to a police station to be charged. They are still debating whether fixed-penalty fines should be available alongside warnings for possession.

The highest category drugs – class A – carry the most severe legal penalties because in theory they are the most harmful. This category includes heroin, cocaine, ecstasy and magic mushrooms. Class B includes speed and barbiturates, while some tranquillisers are in class C.

### Who supports upgrading cannabis again?

Several mental health charities believe reclassification would raise awareness of the links between cannabis use and psychotic illness.

Sane, which gave evidence to the government review, said it knew of hundreds of cases where heavy users of cannabis, particularly skunk, went on to suffer psychotic breakdowns, hallucinations and paranoia.

### Who else objects to reclassification?

Several charities believe another change in the legal status of the drug is unnecessary. The mental health charity Rethink said restoring the drug's class B status was a waste of time and money but it welcomed the government's commitment to a public health campaign.

*7 May 2008*

# Tackling drug crime

## Reducing 'collateral damage' likely to have more impact than big drug hauls, says report

➪ Research published by the UK Drug Policy Commission finds that UK drug markets are extremely resilient and increasing drug seizures has had little street-level impact.

➪ Despite hundreds of millions of pounds spent each year on UK drug enforcement activity, there is remarkably little evidence of its effectiveness in disrupting markets and reducing availability.

➪ The available evidence supports a local partnership approach that focuses on reducing the impact of drug markets as felt by communities.

A review published suggests hopes of substantially reducing or eradicating UK drug markets through enforcement activity alone are unlikely to be fulfilled. Even the most significant drug seizures and dealer/trafficker convictions usually fail to have a sustainable impact on street-level supply and demand due to the scale of the markets and their ability to adapt quickly (for instance by reducing purity levels during periods of short supply).

However, the authors of the review conclude that enforcement agencies can contribute towards reducing the impact of drug markets on communities, for instance by:

➪ tackling markets which cause

the most 'collateral damage' (for instance, those linked with sex markets, human trafficking, gang violence, corruption, drug-related crime and other forms of anti-social behaviour);

⇨ disrupting open street-level markets which affect community confidence, damage neighbourhood reputations and undermine regeneration efforts;

⇨ forming local partnerships to channel users into treatment and related support;

⇨ working closely with local communities to help them become more resilient to drugs (for example, addressing the extent of violence and intimidation in some neighbourhoods);

⇨ tackling emerging markets before they become established;

⇨ recognising and minimising unintended adverse consequences of enforcement (for instance, a local 'crackdown' may just mean dealers move to other neighbourhoods).

David Blakey CBE QPM from the UK Drug Policy Commission said:

'All enforcement agencies aim to reduce drug harms and most have formed local partnerships to do this, but they still tend to be judged by measures of traditional supplyside activity such as seizure rates. This is a pity as it is very difficult to show that increasing drug seizures actually leads to less drug-related harm. Of course, drug dealers must be brought to justice, but we should recognise and encourage the wider role that the police and other law enforcement officials can play in reducing the impact of drug markets on our communities.'

Tim McSweeney, one of the authors of the review, said:

'Within the research literature there is a consistent call for a better understanding of how drug markets operate and the role that enforcement can have in reducing the damage caused by them. We were struck by just how little evidence there is to show that the hundreds of millions of pounds spent on UK enforcement each year has made a sustainable impact and represents value for money, and no published material to allow comparisons of different enforcement approaches.'

The review also shows that:

⇨ the UK illicit drug market is considered one of the most lucrative in the world, worth an estimated £5.3bn – equivalent to around 33% of the UK tobacco market and 41% of the alcohol market. Crack and heroin account for about half the expenditure on drugs;

⇨ £380 million was identified within the UK drug strategy for reducing the supply of drugs in 2005/06 in England but broader criminal justice costs arising from Class A drug use are estimated to be over £4 billion;

⇨ the number of Class A drug seizures in England and Wales more than doubled between 1996 and 2005. The market share (volume) of heroin and cocaine (including crack) seized is estimated to be 12 and 9 per cent respectively;

⇨ however, it has been estimated that between 60% and 80% of drugs would need to be regularly seized to put major traffickers out of business. Seizure rates on this scale have never been achieved in the UK or elsewhere.

*30 July 2008*

⇨ The above press briefing is reprinted with kind permission from the UK Drug Policy Commission. Visit www.ukdpc.org.uk for more information.

© UKDPC

## Public views on cannabis

This poll attempts to gauge the level of public awareness concerning cannabis classification and assess opinions about its reclassification.

**Q1 As far as you understand, what is the <u>current</u> classification of cannabis?**

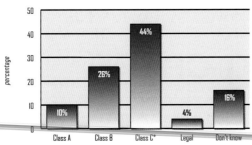

Class A 10%, Class B 26%, Class C* 44%, Legal 4%, Don't know 16%

\* At date of survey, this was the correct answer.

**Q2 And in what class or classification do you think cannabis <u>should</u> be in?**

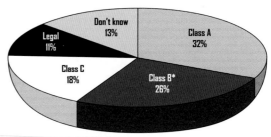

Don't know 13%, Legal 11%, Class C 18%, Class B* 26%, Class A 32%

\* The decision was taken to reclassify cannabis as a Class B substance after research for this survey was undertaken. This will be effectual from January 2009.

**Q3 What do you think the current legal penalty for cannabis possession is?**
**Q4 And what do you think the legal penalty for cannabis possession for personal use should be?**

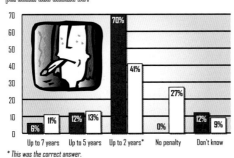

Up to 7 years 6%, Up to 5 years 11%, Up to 2 years* 12% / 70%, No penalty 13% / 41%, Don't know 0% / 27% / 12% / 9%

\* This was the correct answer.

**Q5 Please tell me how strongly you agree or disagree with the following statements? (Graph shows net agree.)**

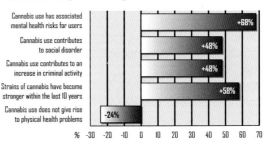

Cannabis use has associated mental health risks for users +68%
Cannabis use contributes to social disorder +48%
Cannabis use contributes to an increase in criminal activity +48%
Strains of cannabis have become stronger within the last 10 years +58%
Cannabis use does not give rise to physical health problems -24%

Source: Ipsos MORI, 'AMCD General Public Polling: Public views in cannabis', 5 February 2008. Results are based on 1,003 telephone interviews with adults aged 16+, conducted between 11 and 13 January 2008.

# Drug smuggling

## Information from HM Revenue and Customs

Illegal drugs can touch the lives of everyone. You might be affected directly if you have a friend or a family member who is a drug user, or indirectly through having to live with the threat of drug-related crime.

Experts estimate the worldwide illegal drugs trade is worth as much as the individual oil, gas or world tourism industries. Whatever the true figure, the UK alone spends more than one billion pounds tackling the problem.

We are committed to working with other agencies such as the Police, National Criminal Intelligence Service and the National Crime Squad to:

⇨ Reducing the supply of illegal drugs.

⇨ Dismantling the criminal gangs that traffic drugs.

⇨ Helping our colleagues around the world tackle illegal drug production and distribution.

⇨ Depriving traffickers of their assets and proceeds of crime.

⇨ Reduce the harm caused by drugs in the community.

### Drug culture

Misuse of Drugs Act 1971 classifies dangerous or otherwise harmful drugs as 'controlled' substances, which means it is illegal to import or export them, possess them, possess them with an intention to supply them to others, or actually supply them without a licence.

These drugs are split into three categories - class A, B and C - according to the threat they pose to a person's health and to society as a whole:

⇨ Class A drugs include those that are widely abused, such as heroin, cocaine ecstasy, LSD and magic mushrooms.

⇨ Class B drugs include amphetamine and speed.

⇨ Class C drugs include cannabis, GHB, anabolic steroids and tranquillisers.

Drugs that do the most harm, such as heroin and cocaine, are the priority of the Government's national drugs strategy.

### Overseas threat

Illegal manufacture of heroin and cocaine is almost unheard of in the UK.

Most of the drugs taken by British users come from thousands of miles away on different continents. They are shipped into our country by well-organised chains of international criminals. For instance, much of the heroin sold in the UK comes from opium poppies grown in Afghanistan.

---

**Experts estimate the worldwide illegal drugs trade is worth as much as the individual oil, gas or world tourism industries**

---

It is processed and moved through 'route countries' such as Turkey, Iran, Pakistan and the Far East before being smuggled into Britain through Europe.

Cocaine is similar but its origins are more likely to be South American. A great deal is routed through the Caribbean and Mexico, then travels through Spain, Portugal, France, Belgium and the Netherlands before making it into the hands of British dealers.

Belgium and the Netherlands are prime sources of synthetic drugs, such as ecstasy and amphetamine; although production of synthetic drugs appears to be on the rise in the UK, too.

The main source countries for cannabis are Morocco, Russia, Pakistan, Lebanon, Colombia, Mexico, Jamaica and Nigeria.

### Smugglers and their techniques

Traffickers try a huge variety of scams to get past our officers. We routinely seize drugs that have been:

⇨ Swallowed or stuffed by someone into their body cavity.

⇨ Hidden on a person.

⇨ Packed into someone's luggage or belongings.

⇨ Stashed in a car, boat or aeroplane.

⇨ Hidden in seemingly legitimate freight.

The effective control of drugs was introduced through legislation such as the Misuse of Drugs Act 1971 which classified dangerous or otherwise harmful drugs to be controlled. Centuries of experience in dealing with smugglers have taught us where some of the biggest risks are and what to look out for.

Our officers develop detailed intelligence, which helps us target attempted smuggling of drugs that follow unusual sea or air routes – yachts that throw huge bundles of drugs overboard in secluded coves, for instance.

Examples of Customs drug seizures for 2002/03 include:

⇨ Heroin – 2,070 kilogrammes.

⇨ Cocaine – 8,767 kilogrammes.

⇨ Ecstasy – 668 kilogrammes.

⇨ Cannabis – 59,034 kilogrammes.

⇨ Number of people sentenced for

drug offences – 1,359
⇨ Average length of sentence – 63 months or approximately five years.

A vital source of help is information from the public to our Customs Confidential Hotline or through HMRC close links to trade organisations.

### The use of guns and violence

Some drugs gangs use the threat of extreme violence to protect their lucrative cargo. It's not just detection which threatens their shipments, but theft by rival criminals.

---

**A kilo of heroin costs less than £1,000 in Pakistan but on British streets it is worth more than 75 times as much**

---

A kilo of heroin costs less than £1,000 in Pakistan but on British streets it is worth more than 75 times as much.

This potential profit has drawn major organised crime syndicates to drug smuggling – the Mafia and Jamaican yardies are known to be involved.

But trafficking also carries massive risks, including some of the most severe international legal penalties.

This means that some drug traffickers are violent and carry guns. It means our officers – who are unarmed – have to work closely with armed police specialists to stop these potentially ruthless criminals.

International co-operation has led to a significant reduction in the number of drug swallowers detected entering the UK. In the year before the UK-Jamaica partnership to deter cocaine-swallowing smuggling – Operation Airbridge – the number of cocaine swallowers detected in the UK had risen rapidly to 730. With the deterrent effect produced by the operation, this number fell dramatically to 185 in the operation's first year up to June 2003, and in the last year up to June 2004, the number has been reduced further to only 41

– a total reduction of more than 90 per cent since the operation began.

### Our officers

Tackling Class A drug smuggling is one of our top priorities. We have units of specialist investigators and dedicated anti-smuggling teams at ports and airports that can deal with any situation quickly and professionally and at a moment's notice 24 hours a day.

But it isn't just on land we operate. Four ships called cutters guard Britain's coastline. Nor is it just humans involved in the anti-trafficking effort. Detector dogs have recorded enormous successes throughout their decades of service.

### The most severe penalties

People who are caught smuggling drugs can be fined a lot of money and sent to prison for a long time.
⇨ Class A – Supply and/or dealing: up to 25 years (life) in prison, an unlimited fine or both.

Possession: up to 7 years' imprisonment, an unlimited fine or both.
⇨ Class B – Supply and/or dealing: up to 14 years in prison, an unlimited fine or both.

Possession: up to 5 years' imprisonment, an unlimited fine or both.
⇨ Class C – Supply and/or dealing: up to 14 years in prison, an unlimited fine or both

Possession: up to 2 years' imprisonment, an unlimited fine or both.

Our powers also allow us to confiscate the criminal's money and possessions if they are the proceeds of their crimes. We are also able to seize any money that we find being moved in or out of the country if we can prove that it is being used for drug smuggling.

⇨ The above information is reprinted with kind permission from HM Revenue and Customs. Visit http://customs.hmrc.gov.uk for more.

---

# Police recorded drug offences

---

### Information from the Home Office

Police recorded drug offences increased by 18 per cent in 2007/08 compared with 2006/07. Increases in recent years have been largely attributable to increases in the recording of possession of cannabis offences which account for 69 per cent of all recorded drug offences. In 2007/08 possession of cannabis increased by 21 per cent, following increases of nine per cent in 2006/07 and 36 per cent in 2005/06. This rise was largely associated with the increased police use of powers to issue warnings for the possession of cannabis. The number of these warnings increased by 28 per cent – a rise of 22,900 detections compared with 2006/07. The increase in possession of other drugs was 15 per cent in 2007/08 compared with the previous year.

The recorded crime figures for possession and trafficking when compared with those from the British Crime Survey for drug use can be seen to significantly understate the true extent of offending in those areas. The statistics will also be heavily influenced by local policing priorities in response to local drug problems, and may reflect changes in the policing of drug crime, such as the use of cannabis warnings, rather than real changes in its incidence.
*July 2008*

⇨ The above information is taken from the report *Crime in England and Wales 2007/2008* and is reprinted with kind permission from the Home Office. Visit www.homeoffice.gov.uk for more information.

# Highs of a world where drugs are legal

### The global legalisation of drugs would raise the Third World out of poverty, says Duncan Campbell

The recent row over the Government's decision to change the classification of cannabis reopened, for a moment, the weary debate over legalisation of drugs. But what would such legalisation really mean?

## Drug trafficking is an estimated $18bn annual business worldwide

What if, a decade from now, the United Nations met to plan their latest drugs strategy, as they will in 2018, and, gazing on events such as the recent drugs-related slaughter in Mexico, the chaos in Afghanistan, the civil war in Colombia, the explosion of crime in Russia, the gulag of 400,000 drug offenders in US jails, decided to legalise the lot – cannabis, cocaine, whatever – across the globe?

At the moment, drug trafficking is an estimated $18bn annual business worldwide. It offers a 2,000 to 3,000 per cent profit margin. Such margins are worth protecting, whether by gun or bribe. What if those margins disappear for the criminal?

In Colombia, in 2018, we might have a negotiated peace with drug money no longer funding either the paramilitaries or Farc and a government no longer embroiled in scandal.

In Afghanistan, we could also have a settlement as poppy farmers, no longer alienated by foreign attempts to deprive them of their living by destroying their crops, might agree to cooperate with the Kabul government. The poppies could be bought for medicinal purposes by the WHO, and pomegranate and almond replacement crops slowly introduced.

In California, the US state with the largest number of drug offenders, there were 21 new prisons and one new university built during a period in the Eighties and Nineties. In 2018, that process could be reversed, with young people being educated in college rather than jail.

If the same happened across the US, it could empower many young black men, who disproportionately make up the prison population, to follow in the footsteps of a recently retired President Obama.

Further south, in Mexico, the legalisation might end the bloody war between gangs and police and inject money into the official economy. In the Caribbean, home to some of the worst per capita violence in the world, the closing down of illicit drug routes might produce profound changes in civic society, with gangs no longer killing each other in drug territory battles.

But what of the scale of the health and addiction problems at home and abroad? There would be a rash of *Daily Mail* stories about dead teenagers, but around the world governments would adjust to the fact that they will – perhaps only briefly – have to invest in health education and rehabilitation programmes with the same enthusiasm with which they once built jails; after all, health ministers now point to the decline in cigarette use in countries where education programmes have been tried.

In the UK in 2008, there were four million problem drinkers and alcohol was implicated in 40,000 deaths each year; there were ten million smokers and tobacco was implicated in 120,000 deaths; there were a million legalised tranquilliser users and 340,000 problematic heroin and crack cocaine users. In 2018, with legalisation, there would be an initial increase in drug use but the billions released into the public purse by legalisation, through taxes on drugs and the emptying of jails and courts, could swiftly be put into use.

Sadly, there will always be casualties; whether drugs are legal or illegal, you cannot make addictive personalities illegal. But there is no need for the economies and political infrastructures of poor countries to be perverted as they are now by the savage effects of keeping drugs illegal.
*10 June 2008*

⇨ The above information is reprinted with kind permission from the First Post. Visit www.thefirstpost.co.uk for more information.
© *First Post*

⇨ Drug-related offences accounted for 3 per cent of all recorded crime in England and Wales in 2005/06. However, drug use can be associated with other forms of criminal activity. For example, an addict may resort to theft if they are unable to pay for drugs. (page 1)

⇨ The 2006/07 BCS estimates that 35.5% of 16- to 59-year-olds have used one or more illicit drugs in their lifetime, 10.0% used one or more illicit drugs in the last year and 5.9% in the last month. (page 7)

⇨ Heavy cannabis use among vulnerable young people can exacerbate existing social problems, such as low educational achievement, homelessness and unemployment, according to a report for the Joseph Rowntree Foundation. However, for others, particularly those in higher or further education, the effects appear to be relatively benign. (page 9)

⇨ According to the Home Office there have been over 200 reported ecstasy-related deaths in the UK since 1996, however, other sources suggest that the drug is 'far safer than aspirin'. (page 9)

⇨ It is estimated that each year in the UK around 114,000 people die from tobacco-related diseases, particularly from cancer, respiratory diseases and heart disease. (page 11)

⇨ The average street price of an ecstasy pill is now only £2.40. (page 13)

⇨ Misuse of over-the-counter pills now kills more Americans than illegal drugs. (page 14)

⇨ Use of the illegal drug ketamine is increasing among young people worldwide, particularly within the electronic dance music scene, according to new research. (page 18)

⇨ Since the government's ten-year drug strategy began in 1998 the cost of drug-related crime has climbed to £100bn, with health costs contributing a further £10bn. Last year alone these costs came to £16.4bn, with each person remaining dependent on illegal drugs costing the country around £44,000 per year. (page 21)

⇨ Over the last decade, use of illegal drugs in the UK has fallen to an 11-year low. Drug-related crime has dropped by a fifth over the last five years. (page 22)

⇨ Between a third and a half of theft and burglary is estimated to be drug-related. (page 23)

⇨ The UK illegal drug market is estimated to be worth between £4bn and £6.6bn a year. (page 23)

⇨ The Government is investing £604 million in drug treatment in 2008/09. (page 24)

⇨ According to the UN World Drug Report 2008, in 2008 there are an estimated 165.5 million users of cannabis products (4 per cent of the world's population between the ages of 15 and 64), compared with 24.7 million users of amphetamines, 16 million users of cocaine, 12 million users of heroin and 9 million users of the psychedelic methamphetamine drug known as ecstasy. (page 25)

⇨ In 2007, 17% of pupils aged 11 to 15 said they had taken drugs in the last year and 10% in the last month. The prevalence of drug use is similar among boys and girls, and increases with age. (page 26)

⇨ Most primary school children are able to name at least four illegal drugs, a new study has shown. (page 27)

⇨ Cannabis supply to young people is largely through social networks and friendship groups rather than through overtly criminal drug markets. This is according to a new study from the Institute for Criminal Policy Research. (page 30)

⇨ A study published in the *Lancet* in spring 2007 concluded UK drugs policy was not fit for purpose. Looking at the harm caused by various narcotic substances, it found alcohol was the fifth most dangerous drug available, following heroin, cocaine, barbiturates and methadone, yet it is not included in the ABC system. Tobacco emerged as the ninth most dangerous drug, ahead of cannabis and the Class A drugs ecstasy and LSD. (page 32)

⇨ Research published by the UK Drug Policy Commission finds that UK drug markets are extremely resilient and increasing drug seizures has had little street-level impact. (page 35)

⇨ Despite hundreds of millions of pounds spent each year on UK drug enforcement activity, there is remarkably little evidence of its effectiveness in disrupting markets and reducing availability. (page 35)

⇨ 32% of respondents surveyed by Ipsos MORI in January 2008 felt that cannabis should be classified as a Class A drug, the most harmful category for illegal substances. 26% felt it should be a Class B substance, while 18% of respondents were happy with the current Class C classification. 11% thought it should be legal. (page 36)

⇨ Drug trafficking is an estimated $18bn annual business worldwide. (page 39)

# GLOSSARY

## Addiction
A dependence on a substance which makes it very difficult to stop taking it. Addiction can be either physical, meaning the user's body has become dependent on the substance and will suffer negative symptoms if the substance is withdrawn, or psychological, meaning a user has no physical need to take a substance, but will experience strong cravings for it if it is withdrawn.

## Amphetamines
Synthetic drugs which can be swallowed, inhaled or injected. Their effects can include increased mental alertness, energy and confidence. Most amphetamines are Class B substances, but crystal meth and prepared-for-injection speed are Class A. Taking amphetamines can cause anxiety or paranoia and risks include overdose and psychological dependence. They can also put strain on a user's heart, leading to cardiac problems.

## Dealing
Supplying drugs to another person, usually in return for money. However, giving drugs away free to friends is also classed as dealing, and is subject to the same penalties as selling drugs. Dealing illegal drugs carries greater penalties than possession for personal use.

## Dependence
A state of reliance on something.

## Depressant
A substance that slows down the nervous system, making the user feel calmer and more relaxed. These drugs are also known as 'downers' and include alcohol, heroin and tranquillisers.

## Drug
A chemical that alters the way the mind and body works. Legal drugs include alcohol, tobacco, caffeine and prescription medicines taken for medical reasons. Illegal drugs taken for recreation include cannabis, cocaine, ecstasy and speed. These illegal substances are divided into three classes – A, B and C – according to the danger they pose to the user and to society (with A being the most dangerous and C being the least).

## Hallucinogen
A drug that causes hallucinations and produces visions and sensations which are detached from reality (a 'trip'). Common hallucinogens include LSD, ketamine and magic mushrooms.

## Misuse of Drugs Act 1971
Prohibits the use of dangerous recreational substances, making it an offence to possess banned drugs for personal use or with the intent to supply. It also divides drugs into three classes, A, B or C, which each have different penalties if you are caught taking or dealing them. Drugs classified as Class A are considered the most harmful and carry the longest prison sentences.

## Opiate
Drugs made from the opium poppy, such as heroin, methadone, opium and morphine.

## Opioid
Synthetic drugs which resemble opiates in their effect. Opioids are available on prescription from doctors, usually for the purpose of pain relief.

## Overdose
This occurs when an individual takes such a large dose of a drug that their body cannot cope with the effects. An overdose can cause organ failure, coma and death.

## Reclassification
When an illegal substance is moved from one drugs class into another, after its harmfulness has been reassessed or new research has uncovered previously-unknown negative effects. Cannabis has been reclassified twice in the past five years, being moved from Class B to Class C in 2004 and back to Class B again in 2009.

## Stimulant
A substance that speeds up the nervous system, making people feel more alert or energised. These drugs are also known as 'uppers' and include caffeine, cocaine, ecstasy and speed.

## Solvent
A volatile substance which gives off fumes. Vapours from products including paint, glue and aerosols can be inhaled and cause intoxication.

## Substance misuse
Substance abuse or misuse is a term which can have different meanings to different people. It can refer to taking drugs or to being dependent on a drug, depending on someone's definition of 'misuse'.

## Tolerance
The way in which the body becomes accustomed to a drug when it is taken repeatedly. This means larger amounts of the drug are needed for it to have the same effect.

## Withdrawal
The symptoms that occur when a person stops taking a drug they are physically dependent on, making the person feel ill and suffer from flu-like symptoms.

# INDEX

# Additional Resources

## Other Issues titles

If you are interested in researching further some of the issues raised in *Drugs in the UK*, you may like to read the following titles in the **Issues** series:

⇨ Vol. 145 *Smoking Trends* (ISBN 978 1 86168 411 0)

⇨ Vol. 143 *Problem Drinking* (ISBN 978 1 86168 409 7)

⇨ Vol. 141 *Mental Health* (ISBN 978 1 86168 407 3)

⇨ Vol. 137 *Crime and Anti-Social Behaviour* (ISBN 978 1 86168 389 2)

⇨ Vol. 136 *Self Harm* (ISBN 978 1 86168 388 5)

⇨ Vol. 128 *The Cannabis Issue* (ISBN 978 1 86168 374 8)

⇨ Vol. 125 *Understanding Depression* (ISBN 978 1 86168 364 9)

⇨ Vol. 123 *Young People and Health* (ISBN 978 1 86168 362 5)

⇨ Vol. 118 *Focus on Sport* (ISBN 978 1 86168 351 9)

⇨ Vol. 100 *Stress and Anxiety* (ISBN 978 1 86168 314 4)

For more information about these titles, visit our website at www.independence.co.uk/publicationslist

## Useful organisations

You may find the websites of the following organisations useful for further research:

⇨ **AddAction:** www.addaction.org.uk

⇨ **Department of Health:** www.dh.gov.uk

⇨ **European Monitoring Centre for Drugs and Drug Addiction:** www.emcdda.europa.eu

⇨ **DrugScope:** www.drugscope.org.uk

⇨ **Economic and Social Research Council:** www.esrcsocietytoday.ac.uk

⇨ **The Home Office:** www.homeoffice.gov.uk

⇨ **Joseph Rowntree Foundation:** www.jrf.org.uk

⇨ **National Treatment Agency for Substance Misuse:** www.nta.nhs.uk

⇨ **NHS Information Centre:** www.ic.nhs.uk

⇨ **Parents Against Drug Abuse:** www.pada.org.uk

⇨ **TheSite:** www.thesite.org

⇨ **UK Drug Policy Commission:** www.ukdpc.org.uk

# ACKNOWLEDGEMENTS

The publisher is grateful for permission to reproduce the following material.

While every care has been taken to trace and acknowledge copyright, the publisher tenders its apology for any accidental infringement or where copyright has proved untraceable. The publisher would be pleased to come to a suitable arrangement in any such case with the rightful owner.

## Chapter One: Drug Trends

*Drugs in the UK*, © Economic and Social Research Council, *Information about common street drugs*, © Parents Against Drug Abuse, *Use of illicit drugs*, © Crown copyright is reproduced with the permission of Her Majesty's Stationery Office, *Heavy cannabis use*, © Joseph Rowntree Foundation, *Can ecstasy kill?*, © TheSite, *Drug deaths*, © DrugScope, *Types of drug-related death*, © Crown copyright is reproduced with the permission of Her Majesty's Stationery Office, *Street drug trends*, © DrugScope, *Legal drug craze is new killer*, © Guardian Newspapers Ltd, *Next year's drug*, © New Statesman Ltd, *Rise in ketamine use among young people*, © University of Bath, *Enslaved by K*, © Guardian Newspapers Ltd, *Cost of UK's illegal drug habit hits £110bn*, © AddAction, *New plan to tackle illegal drugs*, © Crown copyright is reproduced with the permission of Her Majesty's Stationery Office, *The new drugs strategy explained*, © Guardian Newspapers Ltd, *Tackling substance misuse – progress*, © Crown copyright is reproduced with the permission of Her Majesty's Stationery Office, *Drug use worldwide*, © Reuters, *Drug use in Europe*, © European Monitoring Centre for Drugs and Drug Addiction.

## Chapter Two: Young People and Drugs

*Young people and drug use*, © Crown copyright is reproduced with the permission of Her Majesty's Stationery Office, *Primary school kids able to name illegal drugs*, © politics.co.uk, *Dealing with drugs in the schoolyard*, © Telegraph Group Ltd, *Gender differences in drug use*, © The Scotsman, *Supply of cannabis*, © Joseph Rowntree Foundation.

## Chapter Three: Drugs and the Law

*Drugs and politics*, © politics.co.uk, *Drug legislation*, © Parents Against Drug Abuse, *Using harm to classify drugs*, © Medical Research Council, *Q&A: cannabis reclassification*, © Guardian Newspapers Ltd, *Tackling drug crime*, © UK Drug Policy Commission, *Drug smuggling*, © Crown copyright is reproduced with the permission of Her Majesty's Stationery Office, *Police recorded drug offences*, © Crown copyright is reproduced with the permission of Her Majesty's Stationery Office, *Highs of a world where drugs are legal*, © First Post.

## Photographs

**Flickr:** page 29 (Chelsea Oakes).
**Stock Xchng:** pages 15 (Stephen Gibson); 18 (Steve Woods); 24a, 24b (Sanja Gjenero), 26 (Emiliano Spada), 37 (shin0).

## Illustrations

Pages 1, 17, 23, 34: Don Hatcher; pages 7, 20, 28: Angelo Madrid; pages 10, 21, 31, 39: Simon Kneebone; pages 15, 22: Bev Aisbett.

Research and additional editorial by Claire Owen, on behalf of Independence Educational Publishers.

And with thanks to the team: Mary Chapman, Sandra Dennis, Claire Owen and Jan Sunderland.

Lisa Firth
Cambridge
September, 2008

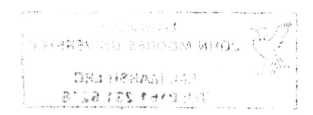